You SHALL RECEIVE
POWER

OTHER TITLES
BY DEREK PRINCE

You
SHALL RECEIVE
POWER

RECEIVING THE PRESENCE
OF THE HOLY SPIRIT
INTO YOUR LIFE

DEREK
PRINCE

WHITAKER
HOUSE

YOU SHALL RECEIVE POWER:
Receiving the Presence of the Holy Spirit into Your Life
Revised and Expanded Edition
(based on the previously published title *Baptism in the Holy Spirit*)

Derek Prince Ministries
P.O. Box 19501
Charlotte, North Carolina 28219
www.derekprince.org

ISBN: 978-0-88368-785-7
Printed in the United States of America
© 1995, 2007 by Derek Prince Ministries, International

Whitaker House
1030 Hunt Valley Circle
New Kensington, PA 15068
www.whitakerhouse.com

Library of Congress Cataloging-in-Publication Data

Prince, Derek.
    You shall receive power : receiving the presence of the Holy Spirit into your life / Derek Prince. — Rev. and expanded ed.
        p. cm.
    ISBN-13: 978-0-88368-785-7 (trade pbk. : alk. paper)
    ISBN-10: 0-88368-785-2 (trade pbk. : alk. paper) 1. Holy Spirit.
    I. Title.
    BT121.3.P76 2006
    234'.13—dc22
                                    2006031512

5 6 7 8 9 10 11 12 **UI** 16 15 14 13 12 11 10

CONTENTS

PART ONE:

BAPTISM IN
the Holy Spirit

Chapter 1

WE WERE ALL BAPTIZED IN One Spirit

WE WERE ALL BAPTIZED IN ONE SPIRIT

*T*he baptism in the Holy Spirit is a topic everyone is talking about. I have traveled and preached quite widely in three different continents, and everywhere I go, I find the baptism is the topic of interest, discussion, and also, perhaps, controversy among Christians around the world.

Sometimes, Christians have the impression that spiritual things are largely a matter of emotion. Thus, they believe they will not have much need for their intelligence. This is a complete mistake.

Instead, we need to give very careful attention to the teaching of God's Word. The information you read here will be of little help to you unless you receive it with your understanding as well as your emotions.

THE UNITY OF THE BODY

The first Scripture I want to look at is in 1 Corinthians:

> *For by one Spirit we were all baptized*
> *into one body; whether Jews or Greeks,*
> *whether slaves or free; and have all been*
> *made to drink into one Spirit.*
>
> (1 Corinthians 12:13)

This verse needs a certain amount of clarification. Trouble has been created for many people regarding it, due to the whims of translators. One prominent feature of the verse is repeated three times. This is the short but important word *one*.

> *Holy Spirit*
>
> God's supreme purpose for bestowing the baptism in the Holy Spirit is the unity of the body of Christ.

We cannot properly appreciate this verse unless we realize that the apostle Paul's main emphasis was not on a doctrine but on the unity of the body of Christ. Those of us who have had the blessing of being baptized in the Spirit have benefited individually through this experience. We need to keep in mind, however, that God's supreme purpose for bestowing it is the unity of the body. Many times we have not been centered in God's line of teaching and revelation because we have strayed from this foundational principle concerning the baptism in the Holy Spirit.

It so happens that I used to be a teacher of Greek at Cambridge University, and I have studied it since I was ten years old. So, in this respect, I dare to say that I know what I'm talking about. I do not doubt that some readers are also familiar with Greek and can turn to any literal translation or commentary to check on the truth of the translation modification I am about to make. I am not asking you to accept the minor modification because of my educational background. Rather, I am asking that you check into it for yourself.

I would say that 1 Corinthians 12:13 could be more accurately translated in this way: "For *in* one Spirit were we all baptized *into* one body,...and we were all given to drink of one Spirit." First, the preposition in the original Greek means "in" and not "by." That so many interpretations of this verse have been based on the word "by" is a minor tragedy.

> *Holy Spirit*
>
> To baptize *into* any condition is to acknowledge the person is already *in* that condition.

13

With regard to the Greek verb *baptizo*, which means "to baptize," there are only two prepositions that ever follow it in the Greek New Testament. One is *en*, which means "in," and the other is *eis*, which means "into." No other prepositions ever follow it anywhere in the New Testament.

"*In* one Spirit," the verse says, "were we all baptized." The verb *baptized* is in the past tense, not the perfect tense, and denotes a single event that took place at a certain moment in our past experience. It is not "we have been baptized," but "we *were* baptized."

THE MEANING OF "BAPTIZED INTO"

In order for us to fully appreciate the meaning of this verse, we need to consider certain parallel passages in the New Testament, particularly with regard to the use of the words *"baptized into,"* which is a rather strange phrase. You have probably met people who say, on the strength of this verse, that unless you have been baptized in the Holy Spirit, you are not a member of the body of Christ. I think this is a terrible thing to say. I respect the sincerity of those who say it, but I think it is a tremendous and basic error.

Thus, before I go further, I want to try to clarify the meaning of 1 Corinthians 12:13 by reference to four other places in the New Testament where the phrase "baptize into" is used. After you look at the passages, I believe you will agree with me that in every case in which "baptize into" is used, the person baptized was already "in" what he was "baptized into."

Baptized into Repentance

The first place where it is used is in Matthew 3:11: "*I indeed baptize you with water unto repentance.*" This is literally "*into* repentance." Does that mean the people whom John baptized had not previously repented or were not in a condition of repentance? Obviously not. This is clear if you look at two preceding verses:

> *But when he saw many of the Pharisees and Sadducees coming to his baptism, he said to them, "Brood of vipers! Who warned you to flee from the wrath to come? Therefore bear fruits worthy of repentance."*
>
> (Matthew 3:7–8)

In other words, John the Baptist was saying, "Demonstrate by your lives that you have repented, and then I'll consider baptizing you."

It is perfectly clear that John baptized people whom he believed had already repented. His baptism of them was outward evidence of his acknowledgment that they had repented; and if he had believed they had not repented, he would not have baptized them.

Baptized into the Remission of Sins

Next, this was the apostle Peter's answer to the question of the convicted multitude after the outpouring of the Holy Spirit on the day of Pentecost:

> *Now when they heard this, they were cut to the heart, and said to Peter and the rest of the apostles, "Men and brethren, what shall we do?" Then Peter said to them, "Repent, and let every one of you be baptized in the name of Jesus Christ for the remission of sins; and you shall receive the gift of the Holy Spirit."* (Acts 2:37–38)

"Be baptized...for the remission of sins" in the Greek is literally "be baptized...*into* the remission of sins." Does this mean their sins were not remitted before they were baptized? No, that would be contrary to the whole of New Testament doctrine.

Their sins were remitted when they repented and put their faith in Jesus Christ. They were then baptized as the outward testimony that the apostles acknowledged they had met the conditions. Once again, they were already in the condition into which they were baptized.

Baptized into Christ

Third, look at the following in Galatians:

> *Therefore the law was our tutor to bring us to Christ, that we might be justified by faith. But after faith has come, we are no longer under a tutor. For you are all sons of God through faith in Christ Jesus. For as many of you as were baptized into Christ have put on Christ.*
>
> (Galatians 3:24–27)

Notice again, the order is clear and decisive. In verse 26, we see that there is only one condition required to make a person a child of God—saving faith in Jesus Christ. Anything that teaches otherwise is a false doctrine. In John 6:47, Jesus said, *"Most assuredly, I say to you, he who believes in Me has everlasting life."* This is more accurately translated as, "He who believes *into* Me has everlasting life." That is the doctrine for which Luther stood—justification by faith alone. Nothing but an active faith in Jesus Christ is required for a person to become a child of God.

Then Paul went on to say, *"For as many of you as were baptized into Christ have put on Christ"* (Galatians 3:27). Notice, they were already *in* Christ; then they were baptized *into* Christ as the acknowledgment that they were *in* Christ.

Baptized into Christ's Death

Last, we read the following in the sixth chapter of Romans:

> *How shall we who died to sin live any longer in it? Or do you not know that as many of us as were baptized into Christ Jesus were baptized into His death? Therefore we were buried with Him through baptism into death, that just as Christ was raised from the dead by the glory of the Father, even so we also should walk in newness of life.* (Romans 6:2–4)

In this passage, we find the phrase *"baptized into"* used in reference to being baptized *into* the death of Jesus Christ. In this sense, Paul also spoke of baptism as a burial when he said, *"We were buried with Him through baptism **into** death."*

It should be perfectly clear that we do not bury a person in order to make him dead. That would be a horrible thought! In fact, our burying a person constitutes our acknowledgment that the person is already dead. Thus, baptism *into* the death of Christ does not in itself produce the condition of being dead to sin in the person baptized; rather, it is the open acknowledgment that the condition has already been produced in that person through faith in the death and resurrection of Christ.

Thus, we have seen the same lesson four times. In each of the cases we have considered, we have found that to baptize a person *into* any condition is to acknowledge publicly that the person is already *in* that condition. In all four cases, the context makes this absolutely plain.

The Baptism Acknowledges Membership and Promotes Unity in the Body

Reading again from Paul's first letter to the church at Corinth, we find,

> *For by one Spirit we were all baptized into one body; whether Jews or Greeks, whether slaves or free; and have all been made to drink into one Spirit.*
>
> (1 Corinthians 12:13)

We can now see the meaning of this passage in its true light. We were already *in* the body. The baptism in the Holy Spirit acknowledges and makes even more public our membership in the body. It also makes more effective our ministry within the body. With the Holy Spirit baptism, we are all *"baptized into"* the oneness of the body. That is the purpose of the baptism in the Spirit. We were already *in* the body just as

YOU SHALL RECEIVE *Power*

the people whom John baptized were already in repentance, just as the people baptized on the day of Pentecost were already in remission of sins, just as the people referred to in Galatians were already in Christ, and just as the people referred to in Romans were already dead to sin before they were buried by baptism into Christ's death.

> *Holy Spirit*
>
> Christ alone can confer the supernatural seal of the baptism in the Holy Spirit.

Thus, we are already in the body of Christ. However, the baptism in the Holy Spirit is a supernatural seal that is given to each individual member by which Jesus Christ acknowledges the member as a part of His body.

Christ alone can confer this supernatural seal. Many different men baptized in water, but John said, *"This is the one who baptizes in the Holy Spirit"* (John 1:33 NASB). There is no one else in all Scripture to whom that privilege is given but Jesus Christ, who thus acknowledges the membership of His body and sets the apostolic seal upon the believers who receive it.

Remember always that the ultimate purpose of the Holy Spirit baptism is the unity of Christ's body. It accomplishes this by making individual members of the body effective agents in bringing about unity—not division—in the body.

Chapter 2

THE NATURE OF
the Experience

THE NATURE OF THE EXPERIENCE

*L*et us now consider the nature of the experience of the baptism as described in the Scriptures and not as people sometimes speak about it in their testimonies.

When I was speaking in Copenhagen, a young man came up to me and said, "I have spoken with other tongues. It happened to me when I was alone. Do you think I have been baptized in the Holy Spirit?"

I said, "Yes, I do. I don't believe any other evidence is required if you have spoken in other tongues as the Holy Spirit gave you utterance."

"Well," he said, "whenever I hear other people speaking about this experience, they always talk about the wonderful emotions they had, the great joy and peace. I didn't feel any special emotion."

I replied, "You can't allow yourself to be led astray by people's testimonies. When the Bible speaks about the baptism in the Holy Spirit, in no case is there any direct reference to any kind of emotion whatever."

Of course, it is a natural instinct in human beings to articulate the way an experience has affected them. If it happened that our emotions were greatly stirred, that is what we will highlight. However, this is *not* what the Bible emphasizes. You may check for yourself that there is no specific reference to emotion in the various places where the baptism in the Holy Spirit is written of and described.

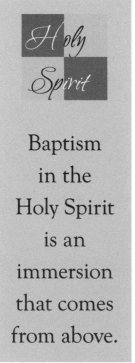

Baptism in the Holy Spirit is an immersion that comes from above.

Don't jump to a wrong conclusion, however. I am not arguing against emotion, because emotion is part of the total human makeup. If a person's emotions are not converted, that person is not fully converted. I certainly believe our emotions should be converted. They should form part of our total Christian experience. But emotions are not an absolute with reference to the baptism in the Holy Spirit.

What does the Bible say about receiving the Holy Spirit? I believe the Bible uses two figures or word pictures. First of all, we read of *baptism*.

In the New Testament, this word is used in connection with the Holy Spirit seven times, which is quite a large number. The other word that is used is *drinking*. If we put these two together, we will form a comprehensive picture from the Scriptures of the experience of the baptism in the Holy Spirit.

A Baptism

Baptism is an immersion, and this immersion comes from above.

I don't want to be controversial, but I spent a day in various libraries at Cambridge University researching the history of the word *baptize*. I traced it from the fifth century before Christ down to the second century of the Christian era. Its definition has never changed. It has always meant "to immerse."

Here we are talking about a baptism not of water but of the Holy Spirit, a coming down of God's Spirit from above over the believer, enveloping him in heaven's atmosphere. This is one aspect of the experience. We read in Acts,

> *When the Day of Pentecost had fully come,* [the disciples and other followers of Jesus] *were all with one accord in one place. And suddenly there came a sound from heaven, as of a rushing mighty wind, and it filled the whole house where they were sitting.*

YOU SHALL RECEIVE *Power*

And suddenly there came a sound from heaven, as of a rushing mighty wind, and it filled the whole house where they were sitting. (Acts 2:1–2)

The whole atmosphere around these believers was filled. They were immersed from above in the supernatural power and presence of God.

Let's move on to a later occurrence:

Now when the apostles who were at Jerusalem heard that Samaria had received the word of God, they sent Peter and John to them, who, when they had come down, prayed for them that they might receive the Holy Spirit. For as yet He had fallen upon none of them. They had only been baptized in the name of the Lord Jesus. Then they laid hands on them, and they received the Holy Spirit. (Acts 8:14–17)

Notice the phrase, *"For as yet He had fallen upon none of them."* The Samaritans' receiving of the Holy Spirit coincided with the Spirit's falling upon them from above.

Then, in the tenth chapter of Acts, Peter was preaching the gospel to Cornelius, a God-fearing Roman centurion, as well as to a number of his relatives and close friends. We read,

While Peter was still speaking these words, the Holy Spirit fell upon all those who heard the word. And those of the circumcision who believed were astonished, as many as came with Peter, because the gift of the Holy Spirit had been poured out on the Gentiles also. For they heard them speak with tongues and magnify God.

(Acts 10:44–46)

Notice that the Holy Spirit *"fell upon"* and was *"poured out"* on them. These phrases describe an immersion coming down from above. The Scripture is very consistent in the descriptive terms it uses.

Peter spoke about this immersion to his colleagues in Jerusalem who had called him to account for his unorthodox behavior in going and preaching to the Gentiles. He told them, in essence, "Well, what could I do? While I was speaking, the Holy Spirit fell on them as He did on us at the beginning. Who was I to resist God?

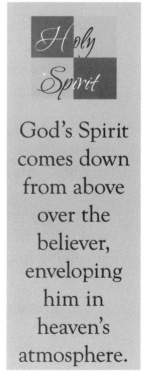

God's Spirit comes down from above over the believer, enveloping him in heaven's atmosphere.

He gave them the same gift that He poured out on us."

So, all these terms are tied together: the baptism, the falling, the receiving, and the gift. They are simply different ways of describing one and the same experience.

A similar occurrence is found in Acts 19, when Paul explained the gospel to the disciples at Ephesus:

> *When they heard this, they were baptized in the name of the Lord Jesus. And when Paul had laid hands on them, the Holy Spirit came upon them, and they spoke with tongues and prophesied.* (Acts 19:5–6)

Notice the phrase *"came upon them."* You can find the same picture described elsewhere, for I have not exhausted the references. However, I have sought to justify this as one primary aspect of the experience. The baptism is a supernatural coming down of the Holy Spirit over the believer, immersing him not in water but in the *shekinah* glory of God's presence.

At this point, I imagine some people might be saying, "The book of Acts is merely historical, so we can't derive doctrines about the baptism in the Spirit from it." Yet the apostle Paul taught,

All Scripture is given by inspiration of God, and is profitable for doctrine, for reproof, for correction, for instruction in righteousness. (2 Timothy 3:16)

"*All Scripture...is profitable for doctrine.*" Since the book of Acts is part of Scripture, it is profitable for doctrine. The Bible presents doctrines in two ways: as statements or commands, and as descriptions of experiences or events. When we combine the two, event and statement meet. We then have a clear picture of what the Bible speaks about because we have all the information.

This concept is analogous to a jigsaw puzzle that you have put together, with the exception of one missing piece. When you find the piece, it fits perfectly, and you click it in place. So it is with the baptism in the Holy Spirit: doctrine, experience, and the events described in the book of Acts all unite, and when you find agreement from every angle, you know you've got it.

A DRINKING

Taking In

The baptism is not merely something that comes down over us, but it is also something that we receive into us. Paul said in 1 Corinthians

12:13 that we *"have all been made to drink into one Spirit."* This ties in exactly with the words of Jesus in John's gospel:

> *On the last day, that great day of the feast, Jesus stood and cried out, saying, "If anyone thirsts, let him come to Me and drink. He who believes in Me, as the Scripture has said, out of his heart will flow rivers of living water." But this He spoke concerning the Spirit, whom those believing in Him would receive; for the Holy Spirit was not yet given, because Jesus was not yet glorified.* (John 7:37–39)

Jesus was referring to the gift of the Holy Spirit for the one who believes, and He compared the receiving of it to the act of drinking. He said, *"If anyone thirsts…,"* which means, "If anyone has a longing in his heart." He then said, *"…let him come to Me and drink,"* which is saying, "Let him receive *into* him."

Flowing Out

At this point, a marvelous miracle takes place as the thirsty person becomes an outlet for rivers of living water. Instead of not having enough for himself, he becomes a channel of supply to many. Relating to others is one of the purposes of the baptism in the Holy Spirit. Maybe you have enough to get you to heaven, but you do not have enough for a needy world. You need the rivers that will flow out of your life.

When I served as a missionary in East Africa, I met many different kinds of people: Africans who had no education or social status, educated Africans, Hindu Asians, Asians who were Muslims, and the white people who, in many cases, regarded themselves as slightly superior to the others. When interacting with all these people, I said, as Paul did in 2 Corinthians 2:16, *"Who is sufficient for these things?"* Who can deal with the almost naked tribesman or the European in his palatial home? How can we truly meet with people? God reminded me of John 7:38: *"Out of his heart will flow* [not a river of living water, but] ***rivers*** *of living water"* (emphasis added). These rivers are enough for everybody.

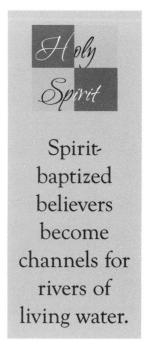

Spirit-baptized believers become channels for rivers of living water.

The outflow of the baptism makes perfectly logical sense. I wrote my fellowship dissertation on logic, and ever since I was converted, I have always rejoiced in the Bible because I find it the most logical book in the world. Its logic is flawless. As far as I am concerned, I have never found an error or a fault in it. Matthew 12:34 says, *"Out of the abundance of the heart the mouth speaks."* When the heart is so full that it can no longer hold its contents, where does it overflow? Through the mouth.

The baptism in the Holy Spirit is a supernatural infilling and a supernatural overflow.

The baptism in the Holy Spirit is a supernatural infilling, and it is a supernatural overflow. How do you know when the vessel is full? It begins to overflow. I cannot see inside your heart or your spirit, and you cannot see inside mine. But, when we see and hear the overflow, we know there has been an infilling.

Today, literally thousands of people are being baptized in the Holy Spirit just as I have described from the Scriptures. The experience of the baptism is clear, logical, scriptural, and practical. If it is not practical, it is not scriptural! Again, where doctrine, biblical events, and personal experience are in agreement, we discover the true nature of the baptism.

Chapter 3

WARNINGS IN
APPROACHING
the Baptism

WARNINGS IN APPROACHING THE BAPTISM

*I*n view of everything we have discussed so far, I want to throw a little cold water on you at this stage. I do not recommend that you seek the baptism in the Holy Spirit or any other spiritual experience unless you are deadly earnest with God. Otherwise, you should stay out of it because your condemnation will be all the greater, and your problems will also be all the greater. Holy Spirit baptism is not an exciting picnic organized by the Sunday school department. We put ourselves in extreme danger if we do not approach it in the right way and if we do not rightly relate it to other aspects of our spiritual experience.

With humility, I want to let you know that I have experienced the baptism and lived in it for well over forty years. In that time, I have seen the wreckage that comes about from a failure to relate the baptism in the Holy Spirit rightly to the rest of the Christian life, experience, and testimony. Let me briefly give you a few words of warning.

BAPTISM IS NOT FORCED

First of all, the Holy Spirit is not a dictator. He is our Comforter and our Teacher. He does not *make* you do things. The person who disturbs a meeting and then says, "I couldn't help it; the Holy Spirit made me do it," has a false picture of the Holy Spirit, because He is *not* a dictator. If a spirit comes into your life and makes you do things, you have the wrong spirit.

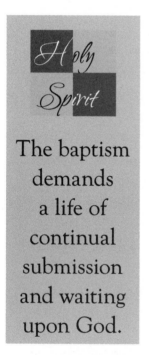

The baptism demands a life of continual submission and waiting upon God.

You will not get any more from the Holy Spirit than you are willing to yield to Him. When some people receive the baptism in the Holy Spirit, they get very little noticeable benefit from it because they are not thereafter willing to be guided, counseled, directed, and controlled by the Holy Spirit. He does *not* force anyone against his will. The baptism demands a life of continual submission and waiting upon God. Somebody has said,

"It is much easier to get filled with the Spirit than it is to stay filled with the Spirit." There is a lot of truth in that.

BAPTISM IS NOT A SUBSTITUTE

Second, the baptism in the Holy Spirit is not a substitute for any other provision of God. God has not given us any one experience that will do everything.

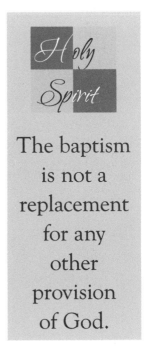

For instance, we read about the Christian armor in the sixth chapter of Ephesians. If you put all six pieces of armor on, you are covered from the crown of your head to the soles of your feet. If, however, you omit one of them, you are no longer fully protected. Suppose you forget the helmet, but you have the shield, the boots, the sword, the belt, and the breastplate. Most of your body is covered, but your head is open to the enemy's attack. The thought life of many Christians is not covered for this reason. They suffer head wounds and lose the power to manipulate the sword and the shield. They have only five pieces when they should have had six.

Holy Spirit

The baptism is not a replacement for any other provision of God.

Here is another example. Some people say, "Well, brother, I've got love. I don't need the gifts." Experience has taught me to question how much love the people who speak like that really have. I would say love is shown mainly in action and not by assertion. Even so, the reasoning is unscriptural because the Bible says we should have both. Love is not a substitute for the gifts of the Spirit, and the gifts of the Spirit are not a substitute for love.

Holy Spirit

Love is shown mainly by our actions and not by our statements.

First Corinthians 12:31 says, *"But covet ["desire" NKJV] earnestly the best gifts: and yet show I unto you a more excellent way"* (KJV), which is the way of love. In a sense, the coveting of the best gifts is a condition of being shown the more excellent way, for a more accurate translation of the verse is, "Covet earnestly the best gifts, *and* I will show you a still more excellent way." First Corinthians 14:1 says, *"Pursue love, **and** desire spiritual gifts"* (emphasis added). This does not say "or desire spiritual gifts." You are not invited to take your choice. You are commanded to pursue both, and if you do not, you are not obeying the Word of God.

BAPTISM USHERS US INTO AN
UNFAMILIAR REALM

Third, the baptism in the Holy Spirit is a spiritual experience, a supernatural experience. In many cases, it is the first supernatural experience many Christians have ever had. As such, it ushers them into a new realm, and often, they are not at home in that realm.

Among other things, it is a realm of spiritual conflict that most of them never knew before they were baptized in the Holy Spirit. Let me give you a little example from the ministry of Jesus. Look at the following:

> *At that time Jesus came from Nazareth in Galilee and was baptized by John in the Jordan. As Jesus was coming up out of the water, he saw heaven being torn open and the Spirit descending on him like a dove. And a voice came from heaven: "You are my Son, whom I love; with you I am well pleased." At once the Spirit sent him out into the desert, and he was in the desert forty days, being tempted by Satan. He was with the wild animals, and angels attended him.* (Mark 1:9–13 NIV)

This is the incident in which Jesus was anointed for His ministry. The Holy Spirit came down on Him and thereafter abode upon Him.

Notice the next thing that happened as a direct consequence of this experience: *"At once the Spirit sent him out into the desert, and he was in the desert forty days, being tempted by Satan."* That is not what humans would expect, but that is spiritual reality. The same kind of thing can happen in your life when you are baptized in the Holy Spirit. You enter into a new spiritual realm in which Satan and the demonic become much more real. Many new avenues into your mind and into your spirit are opened that were not open before. This is not a picnic; it is a reality.

> Holy Spirit baptism often introduces us to the realm of spiritual warfare.

BAPTISM WITHOUT THE WORD IS DANGEROUS

Fourth, the baptism in the Holy Spirit must be united with the Word of God. Otherwise, it is very dangerous. I want you to observe this fact:

Jesus overcame Satan, and He did so with one weapon, the written Word of God.

> *Now when the tempter came to Him [Jesus], he said, "If You are the Son of God, command that these stones become bread." But He answered and said, "It is written, 'Man shall not live by bread alone, but by every word that proceeds from the mouth of God.'" Then the devil took Him up into the holy city, set Him on the pinnacle of the temple, and said to Him, "If You are the Son of God, throw Yourself down. For it is written: 'He shall give His angels charge over you,' and, 'In their hands they shall bear you up, lest you dash your foot against a stone.'" Jesus said to him, "It is written again, 'You shall not tempt the LORD your God.'" Again, the devil took Him up on an exceedingly high mountain, and showed Him all the kingdoms of the world and their glory. And he said to Him, "All these things I will give You if You will fall down and worship me." Then Jesus said to him, "Away with you, Satan! For it is written, 'You shall worship the LORD your God, and Him only you shall serve.'"*
>
> (Matthew 4:3–10)

Three times, Jesus said, *"It is written."* No one needs to know the written Word of God more than a person who has just been baptized in the Holy Spirit. You are in desperate need of studying your Bible and knowing it. Remember that even Satan can quote Scripture, and you have to be able to overcome him not only by being able to quote it better than he does but, more importantly, to be able to choose and wield the right Scripture because you know and understand the Word of God.

Our experiences and actions always need to line up with the Word of God.

Ephesians 6:17 says, *"Take... the sword of the Spirit, which is the word of God."* Notice that the sword of the Holy Spirit is the Word of God, and it is your responsibility to take it. If you take it, the Spirit will wield it through you; but if you do not take it, the Spirit has nothing to use. Oh, the problems that can arise when you are in that defenseless situation!

Let me offer you this final caution in relation to the Word of God: we must not only *know* the Word, but we must be sure to *obey* it. Being baptized in the Holy Spirit is not a license to act in whatever way we wish. Nor is it an excuse for dis-obeying the clear instructions of the Scriptures. Our experiences and actions always need to line up with the Word of God.

Chapter 4

THE PURPOSES OF
the Experience

THE PURPOSES OF THE EXPERIENCE

I have been negative in order to be positive, if I may put it that way. There are a number of important purposes the baptism in the Holy Spirit is intended by God to accomplish in the life of the believer. How much it will accomplish, however, depends on the believer.

GATEWAY TO THE SUPERNATURAL

The following passage contains a great promise if you read it with discernment:

> *For it is impossible for those who were once enlightened, and have tasted the heavenly gift, and have become partakers of the Holy Spirit, and have tasted the good word of God and the powers of the age to come....*
> (Hebrews 6:4–5)

The *"partakers of the Holy Spirit"* have *"tasted"* the powers of the world to come. That is a wonderful description. They have been brought into contact with a power that belongs to the next age but is available to them in this age. In this way, the baptism in the Holy Spirit is intended to be the gateway into the supernatural. It is not a goal; it is a gateway. It is intended by God that thereafter the Spirit-baptized believer should walk in the supernatural. In fact, if I may put it this way, the supernatural should become natural.

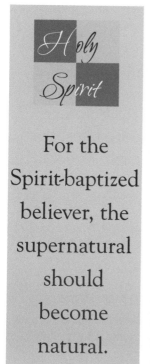

Holy Spirit

For the Spirit-baptized believer, the supernatural should become natural.

Let us look at the book of Acts as a picture of the Christian church. For the sake of intellectual honesty, I offer this challenge: find one chapter out of the twenty-eight in Acts that would be left untouched if all references to the supernatural were removed. Not one of them—not one—would be left intact. We cannot refer to New Testament Christianity without including the supernatural.

I love the reference in Acts that says, *"And God wrought special miracles by the hands of Paul"* (Acts 19:11 KJV). I particularly like the word *"special."* In the original Greek, it means the kind of miracles that do not happen every day. In other words, miracles were an everyday occurrence in the early church, but these were something extraordinary. Even the early church turned around to pay attention to these.

Again, let me say that we can theorize all we want about the New Testament church, but we cannot experience it without the supernatural.

For Witnessing

> *But ye shall receive power, after that the Holy Ghost is come upon you: and ye shall be witnesses unto me.* (Acts 1:8 KJV)

The baptism in the Holy Spirit is intended to clothe us with supernatural power from on high so we can be witnesses. Notice that witnesses are *"unto"* Jesus Christ. They are not unto a doctrine and not primarily unto an experience but unto Jesus Himself. Many of us in the Pentecostal movement have gone astray through becoming witnesses to a denomination, a church, or an experience. However, the true purpose is to witness to Jesus Christ. You will find that the people who use it that way are tremendously successful.

For Prayer

This experience also produces a revolution in a Christian's prayer life. Let's look at Romans for a moment:

> *Likewise the Spirit also helpeth our infir-*
> *mities* ["weaknesses" NKJV]: *for we know*
> *not what we should pray for as we ought:*
> *but the Spirit itself maketh intercession*
> *for us with groanings which cannot be*
> *uttered. And he that searcheth the hearts*
> *knoweth what is the mind of the Spirit,*
> *because he maketh intercession for the*
> *saints according to the will of God.*
> (Romans 8:26–27 KJV)

Notice that we all have an infirmity. It is not a sickness, but it is a natural weakness of the flesh. We do not know how to pray as we ought to pray. Not one person exists who does.

I can say (and I trust I will not be misunderstood) that I have often heard dear brothers in student prayer meetings. I have listened to those sincere, educated young men who studiously pore over their words as they tell almighty God what He ought to be doing.

That is not really prayer. God does not need to be told what to do. Groping with the intellect to find exactly the right thing to tell God to do next is not New Testament prayer; rather, in New Testament prayer, the believer becomes a temple in which a Person comes in and conducts a prayer meeting. That Person is the Holy Spirit. We simply become an instrument.

A certain lady who was born and raised in the Roman Catholic religion in Ireland came to London, where she was saved and baptized in the Holy Spirit. At the time, she worked as a maid in a hotel in London, and she shared a room with another Irish Catholic girl.

One day, the other girl said to her, "I want to ask you something. I hope you don't mind, but every night after you have gone to bed and you seem to be asleep, I hear you talking some foreign language. What is that language?" That young lady got to know for the first time that every night after her body was asleep, the Holy Spirit was praying through her.

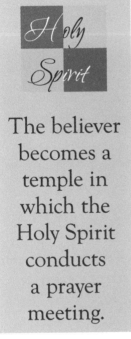

Holy Spirit

The believer becomes a temple in which the Holy Spirit conducts a prayer meeting.

Read what the Scripture says about the bride of Christ: *"I sleep, but my heart is awake"* (Song of Solomon 5:2). That is a spiritual reality. Concerning the fire on the altar of the tabernacle in the Old Testament, it also says, *"A fire shall always be burning on the altar; it shall never go out"* (Leviticus 6:13). That is a picture of the Holy Spirit on the altar of the believer's heart, a fire burning night and day.

Let me show you two other Scriptures, starting with Ephesians 6:18: *"Praying always with all prayer and supplication in the Spirit."* Notice that it says praying *always* in the Spirit. You cannot always pray in your understanding. You cannot always pray in your physical body. But, when the Holy Spirit is there, He doesn't quit.

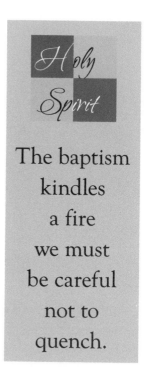

The baptism kindles a fire we must be careful not to quench.

The same thought is found in 1 Thessalonians, chapter five, where it says, *"Pray without ceasing"* (verse 17), and *"Do not quench the Spirit"* (verse 19). These two are related. You can quench the Spirit. You can put the fire out, but it is not God's will. The baptism in the Holy Spirit kindles a fire. Remember that Paul said to Timothy, in essence: "Fan it up again; make it blaze; don't neglect the gift that is in you." (See 1 Timothy 4:14; 2 Timothy 1:6.)

With that same word, I challenge anybody who does not have this supernatural experience because, without it, it is impossible for him to live up to the New Testament standard of prayer. This is what I mean when I say New Testament Christianity is supernatural; it cannot be otherwise.

FOR TEACHING

> *However, when He, the Spirit of truth, has come, He will guide you into all truth; for He will not speak on His own authority, but whatever He hears He will speak; and He will tell you things to come.*
>
> (John 16:13)

> *But the Helper, the Holy Spirit, whom the Father will send in My name, He will teach you all things, and bring to your remembrance all things that I said to you.*
>
> (John 14:26)

The Holy Spirit is the great Teacher of the Scriptures. Jesus Christ promised that when the Spirit of truth came, He would lead us into all truth, teach us, and bring us in remembrance of all Jesus has said.

The Holy Spirit is also the great Revealer of Jesus Christ. Jesus said, *"He will glorify Me"* (John 16:14). These two functions go together because Jesus is the living Word and the Bible is the written Word. The Holy Spirit is the Author of the written Word, and He is the one who comes in to be the Interpreter of the Word.

In 1941, while serving as a soldier in the British army, I was invited by another soldier to attend a Pentecostal service. I had no idea that it was a Pentecostal service, and I did not know then that Pentecostal people existed. I had never heard of them. Had I known anything about them, I might have hesitated to go.

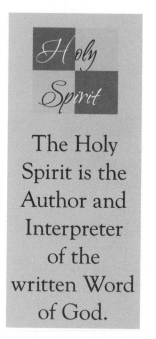

The Holy Spirit is the Author and Interpreter of the written Word of God.

At that time, I had just spent seven years at Cambridge studying philosophy, and I held a fellowship at King's College, Cambridge. If anybody ever went to a religious service with a critical attitude, I was that person. I said to myself, *I'll see whether this preacher really knows what he's talking about.* After I had listened to him for a while, I formed two clear and definite conclusions. The first was that the preacher *did* know what he was talking about, and the second was that I *did not.*

One thing impressed me. As he talked about David, Saul, Samuel, and a whole host of other biblical characters, his relationship to them was such that it seemed as if he had met them that morning. I thought, *Where did he ever get to know these people like that?*

When I was a youth, Bible was a mandatory course at the school I attended. Since I had a fairly accurate memory, I was good at this subject and always scored over 90 percent on tests, even though the classes were rather monotonous. However, that was about fourteen years before this incident. When I was baptized in the Holy Spirit (which happened in an army barracks room shortly after I first heard that Pentecostal preacher), every one of those Bible stories I had studied as a child became as clear and vivid to me as if I had read them the previous day. Who did that? The Holy Spirit. He is the Teacher.

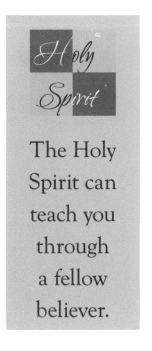

The Holy Spirit can teach you through a fellow believer.

We need human teachers, too, so don't be a fanatic. The Holy Spirit can teach you through another believer. I add that because I have met people who think they do not need to be taught when they have the Holy Spirit. However, He is the Teacher, the Revealer of Jesus Christ. He shows you where Jesus is more clearly than anything else.

Do you know where Christ is? He is seated at the right hand of almighty God, and *"all power is given unto* [Him] *in heaven and in earth"* (Matthew 28:18 KJV). When the Holy Spirit fell on the day of Pentecost, it was like a personal letter from the Lord for those disciples cloistered away in that upper room, saying, "I have arrived; I'm here. You saw Me go; now you know where I am."

Shortly after that, Peter stood up and told those unbelieving, Christ-rejecting Jews,

> *Therefore being exalted to the right hand of God, and having received from the Father the promise of the Holy Spirit, He poured out this which you now see and hear.*
>
> (Acts 2:33)

Peter knew where Jesus was in a new way. Who made that so clear to Him? The Holy Spirit did.

To Exalt Christ

My first wife, Lydia, was a staunch Lutheran in the Danish state church. As a young woman, she was baptized in the Holy Spirit one night in her room. Nobody had pressured her, influenced her, or taught her about it. It was a gift directly from heaven. The change in her life was so dramatic that she did not know what to do, so she went to an elderly, respected pastor in the Lutheran church in Copenhagen. She had heard he was more spiritual than many of the other pastors.

Lydia said, "I wonder whether you can help me. I have a problem."

The pastor was concerned about this young lady who came with a problem. "What is it?" he asked.

"Well," she said, "something has happened to me, but I'm not sure what."

"Can you describe it?" he asked.

"Now, when I pray," she replied, "I feel I'm facing Jesus."

That Lutheran pastor more than thirty years ago replied, "Sister, you must have been baptized in the Holy Spirit."

That's what the baptism in the Holy Spirit is for—to exalt Jesus.

FOR GUIDANCE

Another aspect of the Spirit's ministry is that of guidance and warning.

When He, the Spirit of truth, has come, He will guide you into all truth; for He will

*not speak on His own authority, but what-
ever He hears He will speak; and He will
tell you things to come.*   (John 16:13)

We need that. We need supernatural warning
and direction to survive in the world we live in
today. If we live merely in the natural, we will go
wrong many times.

Spirit-baptized
believers are
ushered into
the councils
of heaven
when they
listen to the
still, small
voice of the
Spirit.

Let me remind you of what
Jesus said in Luke 17:26: *"As it
was in the days of Noah, so it will
be also in the days of the Son of
Man."* We think about the sin
and iniquity that abounded in
the days of Noah, and we say it
is like that today. But remember, there was something else in
Noah's day: *"By faith Noah, being
divinely warned of things not yet
seen, moved with godly fear, prepared an ark for the saving of
his household"* (Hebrews 11:7).
Noah had a supernatural revelation of what was coming on the
earth. He knew the steps to take,
and he knew the way to safety. In
the same way, you and I who are
living in the nuclear age need to have contact with
heaven in a very real and personal way.

Jesus said, *"The Spirit of truth...will not speak on His own authority, but whatever He hears He will speak"* (John 16:13). We are ushered into the councils of heaven when we are baptized in the Holy Spirit and listen to the still, small voice of the Spirit. I can testify personally about this, having traveled many thousands of miles and having been in many lonely and dangerous places. I want to acknowledge the supernatural direction and revelation of the Holy Spirit that has revealed to me many times what was to come next. His guidance has enabled me to take the right action. We definitely need this today.

FOR HEALTH

> *Always carrying about in the body the dying of the Lord Jesus, that the life of Jesus also may be manifested in our body. For we who live are always delivered to death for Jesus' sake, that the life of Jesus also may be manifested in our mortal flesh.* (2 Corinthians 4:10–11)

Notice that the life of Jesus is to be *"**manifested** in our mortal flesh."* Not merely are we to have this invisible, unseen life, but it is to be *visibly* manifested in our bodies. What is the life of Jesus? It is resurrection life, victorious life,

61

powerful life. It is God's will that it should be manifested in our mortal flesh.

What room does this leave for the works of the devil in our bodies? Notice that the word *"manifested"* is used twice in those two verses. In truth, this is divine healing, yet it is more. It is divine health and eternal resurrection life that is now penetrating, operating, and manifesting itself in our mortal bodies.

> *Holy Spirit*
>
> Divine health and eternal resurrection life is now penetrating, operating, and manifesting in our mortal bodies.

Who is the Administrator of this life? The answer is in Romans 8:10: *"And if Christ is in you, the body is dead because of sin, but the Spirit is life because of righteousness."* Isn't that wonderful?

The night I got saved, I didn't know anything about the doctrine of salvation. After all, I had been educated at Eton College and King's College, Cambridge, so what would I know about salvation? I say that jokingly, but it is a sad thing. However, it is a fact that up to the age of twenty-five, I had never heard the gospel preached. I had never met a person who could testify to a personal experience of being born again.

People talk about darkest Africa, but I have never met an African who was in grosser spiritual darkness than I was after seven years at Cambridge. At that time, I was a habitual, inveterate blasphemer, and I was also an extremely heavy drinker. I did not know what salvation was, but a moment came when I knew that I had met people who had something I did not have. I reasoned that God could not be unfair, so if He gave it to them, He must give it to me.

I asked Him for it and got it sometime after midnight in an army barracks room. The next day, I no longer blasphemed. Also, when I went to the pub to buy a drink, it was almost as if my legs would not walk inside. I was under new Management. I did not even want a drink, and it was only habit that took me to that place.

> *Holy Spirit*
>
> I was under new Management. I did not even want a drink!

What broke the power of blasphemy and drink like that? Christ had come in, and the old body was dead. A dead body does not lust for drink. A dead body does not blaspheme. A new life had come in. What life? *"The Spirit is life because of righteousness"* (Romans 8:10). Being justified by faith in Jesus Christ, we have access to a new life. The Spirit comes in and gives us *"life because of righteousness."*

Continuing to read in Romans, we find,

> *But if the Spirit of Him who raised Jesus from the dead dwells in you, He who raised Christ from the dead will also give life to your mortal bodies through His Spirit who dwells in you.* (Romans 8:11)

That is the Holy Spirit, the Administrator of the resurrection life of Jesus, imparting it to our mortal bodies.

Not coincidentally, almost everywhere that people are baptized in the Holy Spirit, they begin to pray for the sick. I can scarcely think of an exception. I know there are some who are not baptized in the Holy Spirit, yet they have seen prayer for healing in the Scriptures and faithfully practice it. God honors their prayers. God did it for the disciples, too, even before the day of Pentecost. We read that the disciples went out during the earthly ministry of Jesus and anointed many of the sick with oil. They also cast out demons. So, God will honor those who pray for the sick even if they have not received the baptism.

Nevertheless, it is a fact that wherever the Holy Spirit has come in as the Administrator of divine life from Jesus Christ, almost instantly, He illuminates the eyes of God's people to see that this life is not merely for the inward man but for the outward man as well. Almost inevitably, you will find that this happens.

FOR UNITY

Finally, I return to my initial text:

For [in] *one Spirit we were all baptized into one body; whether Jews or Greeks, whether slaves or free; and have all been made to drink into one Spirit.*

(1 Corinthians 12:13)

Remember this: the ultimate purpose of God in baptizing believers in the Holy Spirit is to unite them and not to separate them.

Somebody complained about a certain church in the United States where the minister had been baptized in the Holy Spirit. Some of the congregation had gone along with him while others had not. The person said, "The trouble with this experience is that it is dividing the church." To this dubious statement, another minister, whom I know personally, responded with this excellent answer: "That's remarkable, because in the early church it had exactly the opposite effect. When the Jews heard the Gentiles speak with other tongues, it was the only thing that united Jews and Gentiles in one church and one body. Nothing else would have done it."

The baptism brings diverse Christians together in unity, fellowship, and worship.

Likewise, the only thing that will bring Baptists, Plymouth Brethren, Assemblies of God members, Anglicans, Lutherans, Presbyterians, and many other denominations together in large numbers—embracing one another, throwing their arms up in the air, spending time doing nothing but praising God—is the baptism in the Holy Spirit.

Let me tell you of an incident that made a deep impression on me. I was speaking at a convention of the Full Gospel Businessmen's Fellowship in Spokane, Washington. It was held in a big hotel where several hundred people were present. I was teaching the afternoon Bible study, especially warning those in attendance about the dangers of fooling around with Pentecost.

When I came to the end of my message, I did not know what to do since they had no specified program, and so I just stood there and was silent. Soon a lady began to sing in an unknown tongue. I would describe it as a kind of Gregorian chant. It so happened that the brother who was with me on the platform was a choir leader and quite an expert in music. When she had finished singing, he said, "That was a very complicated melody." We waited a little while, and a young man began to sing in English. He gave the interpretation of that song, singing in exactly the same melody. The words that he sang also fit the melody. The man beside me said, "He kept the melody perfectly." In the course of the day, this happened twice.

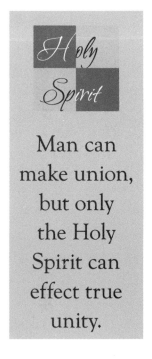

Man can make union, but only the Holy Spirit can effect true unity.

The interesting part of this whole story is that I did something we do not often do at these conventions. We rarely ask others what their denominational affiliations are, since we are not concerned about particular labels. However, because it seemed to tie in so perfectly with the subject at hand, I made some inquiries about the denominational alliances of these two people. I discovered that the lady was a Lutheran and the young man was an Episcopalian. However, we were all one in Jesus Christ in the unity of the Holy Spirit.

Today, the church of Jesus Christ faces two alternatives. On the one hand, we have *union,* and on the other, we have *unity.* I will not go so far as to say that these two are mutually exclusive. However, though man can make union, only the Holy Spirit can make unity.

Chapter 5

THE SCRIPTURAL PATTERN FOR RECEIVING THE Holy Spirit

THE SCRIPTURAL PATTERN FOR RECEIVING THE HOLY SPIRIT

I f we are to live in the fullness of the baptism in the Holy Spirit, we need to understand who the Holy Spirit is and how to receive Him.

Throughout the Scriptures, we are given many pictures of the Holy Spirit that are drawn from everyday life, and most of these pictures are nonpersonal. The Holy Spirit is typified by wind, fire, rain, dew, and oil, to name only five things.

Particularly in the New Testament, we find a special emphasis on the word *He* in reference to the Spirit, bringing into focus the fact that the Holy Spirit is legitimately a Person. So we need the understanding of the whole Bible to help us learn and receive the totality of the Spirit's nature and work.

Jesus' Main Ministry Was to Baptize in the Holy Spirit

Let us read the words with which John the Baptist introduced the Messiah, the Christ:

> *"I did not know Him* [John knew Jesus as his cousin, but he didn't yet know Him as the Messiah]; *but that He should be revealed to Israel, therefore I came baptizing with water." And John bore witness, saying, "I saw the Spirit descending from heaven like a dove, and He remained upon Him. I did not know Him, but He who sent me to baptize with water said to me, 'Upon whom you see the Spirit descending, and remaining on Him, this is He who baptizes with the Holy Spirit.' And I have seen and testified that this is the Son of God."*
> (John 1:31–34)

The whole purpose of John the Baptist's ministry was to prepare the way for Jesus, and he had to do one specific thing: he had to baptize people in water. I think that not only his words, but also his acts, were prophetic. He was saying, in effect, "What I am doing in water, the One who comes after me will do in the Holy Spirit."

And so Jesus was introduced as the One who baptizes in the Holy Spirit. This introduction is found in all four gospels, Matthew, Mark, Luke, and John. God intended Jesus to be presented to Israel not primarily as the Savior, not primarily as the Lamb of God, but as the One who baptizes in the Holy Spirit. This was the main aspect of Jesus' ministry that John emphasized, and yet, strangely enough, most of the church for many centuries has hardly given any attention to it whatever.

JESUS' TEACHING REGARDING THE HOLY SPIRIT

Let us look at the actual teaching of Jesus in relation to the Holy Spirit, beginning with a passage we looked at earlier in this book:

> *On the last day, that great day of the feast, Jesus stood and cried out, saying, "If anyone thirsts, let him come to Me and drink. He who believes in Me, as the Scripture has said, out of his heart will flow rivers of living water." But this He spoke concerning the Spirit, **whom those believing in Him** would receive; for the Holy Spirit was not yet given, because Jesus was not yet glorified.*
>
> (John 7:37–39, emphasis added)

Jesus was speaking about something that was yet in the future. It is not correct to apply this passage to the conversion of sinners, but to believers receiving the Holy Spirit. John 7:39 says, *"For the Holy Spirit was not yet given."* The word *"given"* is in italics in several Bible translations because it is supplied by the translators. The original Greek actually says, "The Holy Spirit was not yet." Obviously, this doesn't mean that the Holy Spirit was not yet in existence, so the translators had to decide how they were going to phrase it. I think one word we could use is *available*. The Holy Spirit was not yet available. What Jesus was talking about could not happen until He had returned to heaven and been glorified once again at the right hand of the Father. So, although the promise was given in John 7, its fulfillment did not come until Acts 2, after Jesus had been glorified.

> *Holy Spirit*
>
> The promise of the Spirit was fulfilled after Jesus had been glorified by the Father.

AN EXCHANGE OF PERSONS

As Jesus began to draw near to the close of His earthly ministry, He began systematically to prepare His disciples for the fact that He was going to leave them, but that another Person would come to take His place. It is at this point in the teaching of Jesus that the Holy Spirit as a Person is most strongly emphasized. The essence of what Jesus was saying was that there was to be an exchange of persons. "I, the Son of God, as a Person, am going away. In My place, another Person, the Holy Spirit, will come."

Comforter

> *If ye love me, keep my commandments. And I will pray the Father, and he shall give you another Comforter, that he may abide with you for ever.*   (John 14:15–16 KJV)

Jesus was saying, "I'm going to ask the Father to meet your need. When I go away, He'll give you another Comforter." What does the word *"another"* indicate? There are two Greek words for another. One means different in number, and the other means different in kind. The word used here is different in number. The divine Person Jesus was going, but He would ask the Father to send another divine Person in His place, and that Person was the Comforter.

As the Comforter, the Holy Spirit is an encourager; He never discourages the children of God. You need to bear in mind that any kind of influence that discourages you is not from the Holy Spirit. If you sin, He will reprove you specifically and tell you what to do, but He will never discourage you. Many people have discouraging influences in their lives, and they think it's the Holy Spirit, but it isn't. He is the Encourager, not the discourager.

Spirit of Truth

In the next verse, Jesus called the Holy Spirit the Spirit of truth:

> *The Spirit of truth, whom the world cannot receive, because it neither sees Him nor knows Him.* (John 14:17)

Note again that we are not talking about something that sinners receive. As Jesus said, "The world can't receive this." This is something that born-again children of God can receive, but sinners can't because they are not in contact with Him. They don't see Him, they don't know Him, they don't understand Him, and He's not real to them.

Ever Present Provider

> *But you know Him, for He dwells with you and will be in you. I will not leave you orphans; I will come to you.*
> (John 14:17–18)

Without the Holy Spirit, we Christians would be like orphans. Jesus was saying, in effect, "I will not leave you as orphans without anybody to care for you, teach you, comfort you, or provide for you. When I go, another Person will come." Through the Holy Spirit, we don't have to be orphans if we accept Jesus' provision for us.

Jesus said, *"And he shall give you another Comforter, that he may abide with you for ever"* (verse 16 KJV). The word *forever* is significant. Jesus as a Person had been with His disciples for only three-and-a-half years. Now He was leaving them just when they were really getting to know Him. But He said that the next Person who came would never leave them. He would come to stay forever. That is the Holy Spirit.

Teacher

Then, in John 14:25–26, Jesus said,

> *These things have I spoken unto you, being yet present with you. But the Comforter, which is the Holy Ghost, whom the Father will send in my name, he shall teach you all things, and bring all things to your remembrance, whatsoever I have said unto you.* (KJV)

We talked in the previous chapter about the role of the Holy Spirit as Teacher. I am impressed by the confidence Jesus had in the Holy Spirit. I think we need to have an equal confidence. Sometimes we think we have to do the whole job and that, if we won't do it, it won't get done. Yet Jesus said, "I've done what I can do. When the Holy Spirit comes, He'll finish the job." I really think that was a mark of humility on Jesus' part.

I'm learning what God expects me to do and what I'm to leave to the Holy Spirit. If I think I have to do it all, it's usually a failure. But Jesus said, "I've taken you as far as you're able to come now. I can't give you any more because you can't receive it. It would be wasting words on you." Pouring water into a bottle with a cap on it is a waste. So He said, "I'm leaving you, but it will be all right because when the Holy Spirit comes, I have absolute confidence in Him. He'll finish the job."

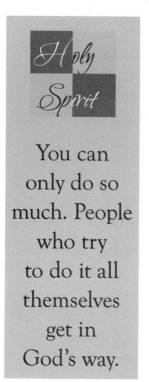

Holy Spirit

You can only do so much. People who try to do it all themselves get in God's way.

I really think that if you are the leader of any kind of discipleship program, you need to bear that in mind. You can do only so much; the Holy Spirit will have to do the rest. People who try to do it all get in God's way. Jesus never got in the way of the Father. He knew when to leave a situation. My late wife, Lydia, used to say, "Always leave when you're on the peak. Never wait until the thing fizzles out." That is very good advice. Some people only leave when the whole thing has fallen apart, and there's no alternative, so they say, "Well, God's calling me elsewhere." There is a real art in knowing when to leave. It is being sensitive to the Holy Spirit. Therefore, Jesus said, "I've done what I can, but another Teacher is coming. He's going to do two things. He's going to teach you what I haven't yet taught you, and He's going to bring everything I have taught you to your remembrance."

Teacher and Remembrancer are two of the Holy Spirit's great ministries. The record of the Scriptures does not depend merely on the fallibility of human memory. The Holy Spirit came to make sure the biblical authors got the record absolutely correct. He brought all things to their remembrance. We can rely on it because it is a Spirit-inspired record.

> *Holy Spirit*
>
> One reason the Holy Spirit came was to make sure the biblical authors got the record absolutely correct.

The Holy Spirit also gave the New Testament authors understanding of many events they might not otherwise have recorded, because they wouldn't have seen the significance of them. For example, suppose you were to try to describe any event that happened in your life even a year ago. Or suppose you had to get six people who were present at the same event to sit down and individually write their accounts of what happened. You'd hardly know some of them were describing the same event. It's not easy, but the disciples did not have to depend merely on human ability. They were promised that the Holy Spirit would bring all things to their remembrance.

An Expedient Exchange

As Jesus continued the process of instruction and preparation of His disciples for His leaving, He said,

> *But now I go away to Him who sent Me, and none of you asks Me, "Where are You going?" But because I have said these things to you, sorrow has filled your heart.* (John 16:5–6)

They just couldn't grasp anything but the awful fact that Jesus was leaving, but He said something very significant that we need to understand:

> *Nevertheless I tell you the truth. It is to your advantage that I go away; for if I do*

> *not go away, the Helper [*"Comforter"* KJV]*
> *will not come to you; but if I depart, I will*
> *send Him to you.*   (John 16:7)

> *I still have many things to say to you, but*
> *you cannot bear them now. However, when*
> *He, the Spirit of truth, has come, He will*
> *guide you into all truth.*   (John 16:12–13)

Here again is the principle of the exchange of Persons. Jesus said, "As long as I'm here, the Comforter won't come. But if I leave, then I'll be free to send the Comforter to take My place. This is expedient for you; it's in your best interests." I believe He was saying, "You'll be better off with Me in heaven and the Holy Spirit on earth, than you are now with Me on earth and the Spirit in heaven."

Holy Spirit

When the Spirit came, the disciples had a new perspective on the life and ministry of Jesus.

It is very obvious that this proved true because the moment the Holy Spirit came, the disciples had an entirely different understanding of the whole life, ministry, and teaching of Jesus. Up to that time, they were extremely slow to appreciate even the basic truths that Jesus was saying. The moment the Holy Spirit came, they had a totally different grasp.

Many times, we hear Christians say, "Wouldn't it be wonderful if we were like the apostles in the days of Jesus' earthly ministry—if we were as close to Jesus as that and had that amount of teaching from Him?" But that's not what the Scripture teaches. John 16:7 tells us we are better off now than the disciples were during the period when Jesus was on earth and the Holy Spirit had not yet come. The Holy Spirit could not come while Jesus was personally present on earth.

> *When He, the Spirit of truth, has come, He will guide you into all truth; for He will not speak on His own authority, but whatever He hears He will speak; and He will tell you things to come.* (John 16:13)

When we have the Holy Spirit, we can say reverently that we have a private line to heaven. We can be informed of what is going on in the counsels of the Godhead.

In the above verse, we have one of the clearest indications of the personality of the Holy Spirit. *"When He, the Spirit of truth, has come...."* Notice that the pronoun is *He,* not *it.* In the Greek, the word for *"Spirit,"* which is *pneuma,* is neuter. The

Greek language has three genders: masculine, feminine, and neuter. The pronoun that should be used here, to be grammatically correct, would be *it*. But Jesus, or the writer of the gospel, John, deliberately broke the rules of grammar to use the masculine pronoun *he*, not the neuter pronoun *it*. That's as emphatic a way as possible to say that the Holy Spirit is a He.

THE HOLY SPIRIT GLORIFIES JESUS

> *He will glorify Me, for He will take of what is Mine and declare it to you.*
> (John 16:14)

The Holy Spirit never glorifies Himself; He glorifies Jesus. He never focuses on Himself; He focuses on Jesus. Everything the Holy Spirit does is ultimately directed to glorifying Jesus, so anything that does not essentially glorify Him is not a work of the Holy Spirit. That is one good way to test what is of the Spirit.

THE HOLY SPIRIT IS THE ADMINISTRATOR OF OUR ETERNAL INHERITANCE

The next fact Jesus revealed is that the Holy Spirit is the Administrator of our inheritance.

> *All things that the Father has are Mine. Therefore I said that He will take of Mine and declare it to you.*　　(John 16:15)

Everything that the Father has belongs to the Son, and everything the Son has belongs to the Father, and the Holy Spirit is the Revelator and Administrator of all of it. Romans 8:17 tells us that we are *"heirs of God and joint heirs with Christ."* We can legally share the whole inheritance with Jesus Christ. But the important thing to remember is this: the Holy Spirit administers the inheritance. Jesus was saying, "I've made the Holy Spirit My Executor. If you want the inheritance, see the Executor."

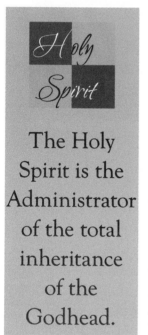

The Holy Spirit is the Administrator of the total inheritance of the Godhead.

This point is very vividly illustrated in Genesis 24 in the story of Abraham obtaining a bride for his son, Isaac. Abraham is a type of God the Father, Isaac is a type of Jesus Christ the Son, and Rebekah is a type of the church. There's one more person in the story, and that's the servant, who represents the Holy Spirit. If you read the story for yourself, you will find it states specifically that everything Abraham and Isaac owned was under the control of the servant. The servant administered the entire inheritance. Likewise, the Holy Spirit is the Administrator of the total inheritance of the Godhead.

The reason some Christians have so much in theory but so little in experience is that they have read the will, but they haven't become acquainted with the legal Executor. The Holy Spirit takes everything that belongs to the Father and the Son, reveals it, and imparts it to us. If you bypass the Executor, you don't get anything in the will.

Christianity can never be reduced merely to a kind of theology because theology is the will. You can hold the will in your hand forever and have nothing of the inheritance. The closer you are to the Holy Spirit, the more you will enjoy of your inheritance. But if you are not in right relationship with the Holy Spirit, you are going to be living like an orphan when you should be living like the child of a king. The inheritance is there, but you will be unable to access it.

RECEIVING THE INBREATHED SPIRIT

I now want to discuss what it meant for Jesus' disciples to receive the inbreathed Spirit. The day Jesus was resurrected, He appeared to the disciples as a group.

Then, the same day at evening, being the first day of the week, when the doors were

> *shut where the disciples were assembled,*
> *for fear of the Jews, Jesus came and stood*
> *in the midst, and said to them "Peace be*
> *with you." When He had said this, He*
> *showed them His hands and His side.*
> (John 20:19–20)

Though His body had been wonderfully transformed, it still retained the visible marks of His crucifixion as indisputable evidence of the fact that He was the very same Person whom they had seen crucified and die on the cross. We read,

> *Then the disciples were glad when they*
> *saw the Lord.* (John 20:20)

I am sure that tremendous, indescribable joy filled their hearts when they really grasped the fact that He was alive.

> *So Jesus said to them again, "Peace to*
> *you! As the Father has sent Me, I also*
> *send you." And when He had said this,*
> ***He breathed on them**, and said to them,*
> ***"Receive the Holy Spirit."***
> (John 20:21–22, emphasis added)

"He breathed on them." The Greek word for *"breathed"* is used in secular Greek of a flute player breathing into the mouth of his flute to produce music. And a person who is playing a flute

or any similar instrument does not stand at a distance and blow at it. He brings it right up to his mouth and fits his mouth to the mouthpiece and blows into it. Now I cannot prove this, and I'm not attempting to, but to me the implication is that Jesus did not stand and breathe at the disciples in a group but came to each one individually and breathed into him.

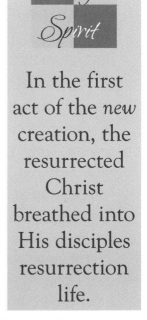

I believe it occurred this way because this was the new creation, and it was a kind of replay of when man was first created in the garden. The Lord God had stooped down, put His lips against those lips of clay, and breathed into Adam the breath of life. Likewise, in the first act of the *new* creation, the resurrected Christ breathed into His disciples not just life, but resurrection life.

In the first act of the *new* creation, the resurrected Christ breathed into His disciples resurrection life.

I believe there is a great difference between the breath of life Adam received and the breath the disciples received. This was life that had triumphed over death. This was eternal life. Indestructible life. Life that neither sin, death, Satan, nor anything else could ever conquer or overcome.

He breathed into them totally victorious life, His own life. And He said, *"Receive the Holy Spirit."*

In the Greek, the definite article *the* is not there. Bear in mind that the word translated *"Spirit,"* which is *pneuma*, also means breath or wind. So we might legitimately translate this as, "Receive holy breath." And I believe His action went with His words. He breathed into them holy breath, divine resurrection life breath, and they were created anew. This is the moment when the new creation took place for the first time.

I believe that, at this time, the disciples were saved with what we would call New Testament salvation. Romans 10:9 says that in order to receive New Testament salvation, two acts are required: you have to confess Jesus as Lord, and you have to believe in your heart that God raised Him from the dead. Without these two steps, you can have the kind of salvation they had in the Old Testament—an anticipation of what Christ was to purchase—but you cannot have actual salvation. When Jesus breathed upon His disciples, I think this was the first time they believed in their hearts that God had raised Him from the dead.

The disciples received the Holy Spirit not primarily as a Person, but as breath, as divine resurrection eternal life. They received the resurrected Christ and the inbreathed Spirit. But the promises Jesus had given in John's gospel all the way through, which we have traced, were not yet fulfilled.

THE OUTPOURING OF THE SPIRIT

The fact that the promise of the Holy Spirit had not yet been fulfilled is very important to understand because, forty days later, Jesus still referred to those promises as being in the future. Let us turn to the book of Acts, to the time just before Jesus ascended to heaven, when He told His disciples,

For John truly baptized with water, but you shall be baptized with the Holy Spirit not many days from now.   (Acts 1:5)

But you shall receive power when the Holy Spirit has come upon you.   (Acts 1:8)

In his gospel, Luke also recorded these instructions of Jesus to His disciples just before He ascended,

Behold, I send the Promise of My Father upon you; but tarry in the city of Jerusalem until you are endued with power from on high.   (Luke 24:49)

At that time, being baptized with the Holy Spirit was still in the future. The Scripture reveals the fulfillment of the *"not many days from now"* that Jesus spoke of in Acts 1:5. Ten days later, on the day of Pentecost, the disciples had the experience that Jesus had been promising. Almost all commentators on the New Testament, whether they're Catholic or Protestant, Baptist or Pentecostal, agree that the day of Pentecost was the fulfillment of the promises that Jesus gave all through the gospel of John.

Let's look at this experience as it is described in Acts 2.

> *When the Day of Pentecost had fully come, they were all with one accord in one place. And suddenly there came a sound from heaven, as of a rushing mighty wind, and it filled the whole house where they were sitting. Then there appeared to them divided tongues, as of fire, and one sat upon each of them. And they were all filled with the Holy Spirit and began to speak with other tongues, as the Spirit gave them utterance.* (Acts 2:1–4)

A little while later, Peter explained to the crowd that had gathered, *"This is what was spoken by the prophet Joel: 'And it shall come to pass in the last days, says God, that I will pour out of My Spirit on all flesh'"* (Acts 2:16–17). These words show us what we are dealing with here. This was the promise. Peter explained that the Holy Spirit was given because Jesus had been glorified.

> *This Jesus God has raised up, of which we are all witnesses. Therefore being exalted to the right hand of God, and having received from the Father the promise of the Holy Spirit, He poured out this which you now see and hear.* (Acts 2:32–33)

This was the culmination of all those promises. When Jesus was glorified in heaven, He received from the Father the promise of the Spirit and then poured out the Holy Spirit on the waiting disciples. What we are talking about in receiving the baptism in the Holy Spirit is the same experience the disciples received on the day of Pentecost.

IMMERSION, INFILLING, AND OUTFLOW

What do we see in the disciples' experience described above? My analytical mind sees three things: (1) an immersion or a baptism; (2) an infilling; and (3) an outflow. I believe that is the package deal. You can take away from it and still have something, but you won't have what the disciples experienced.

I believe the baptism in the Holy Spirit is an immersion. There are two kinds of immersion.

I call them the swimming pool immersion and the Niagara Falls immersion. Water baptism is a going down into and a coming up out of. That is the swimming pool immersion. The baptism of the Holy Spirit is the Niagara Falls immersion. I remember once standing and looking at Niagara Falls as that great volume of water cascaded over the cliff. I thought to myself, *You wouldn't be under that water for half a second without being totally immersed.* It comes down over from above. It envelops and surrounds. Every place in the first fifteen chapters of the book of Acts where it talks about the Holy Spirit coming on people, the language always implies a coming on them from above.

The baptism in the Holy Spirit is a "Niagara Falls" immersion—it comes down from above, enveloping the believer.

So on the day of Pentecost, there was an immersion. The Spirit of God came down from heaven over the followers of Jesus, and it filled the whole house where they were. Since the whole house was filled, every one of them was individually immersed in the presence of the Holy Spirit. That is absolutely inescapable.

Second, it says, *"They were all filled"* (Acts 2:4). It did not merely surround them, but it also came into them; they were internally filled.

Third, having been filled, it says they *"began to speak"* (verse 4). That's the outflow. Remember that Matthew 12:34 says, *"Out of the abundance of the heart the mouth speaks."* When the heart is filled to overflowing, the overflow takes place through the mouth in speech. When did they know they were filled? When they overflowed. Up to that moment, there was no way they could measure just how "high" the infilling had come. But when it overflowed, they knew they had been filled.

THE SCRIPTURAL PATTERN

I believe this is the scriptural pattern for receiving the baptism in the Holy Spirit. My experience is that if we teach people this pattern, this is what they receive. If we teach less than this, people tend to receive less. I see no reason to reduce what God has presented: the immersion, the infilling, and the outflow.

Perhaps you have never been baptized in the Holy Spirit. If you become convinced in your heart that this is the experience you are to receive, you can receive it. The moment you believe that it will happen, it will happen.

The Scriptures record that many people who witnessed the immediate results of the baptism in the Spirit didn't understand what was occurring. Some of us have had the same experience.

As I mentioned earlier, in 1941, when I was a soldier in the British army, the Lord miraculously visited me in the middle of the night in a barracks room, revealed Jesus to me, and about ten days later baptized me in the Holy Spirit. I began to speak in an unknown tongue for the first time in that barracks room.

> *Holy Spirit*
>
> When the heart is filled to overflowing, the overflow takes place through the mouth in speech.

I shared the room with one other soldier, and the night I was converted, he awakened to find me lying on my back in the middle of the floor. He walked around me at a distance shaking his head and saying, "I don't know what to do with you. I suppose it's no good pouring water over you."

The night God baptized me in the Holy Spirit, this soldier was out at a dance. After I had been speaking in tongues for about ten minutes and still wasn't very sure what it was all about, I heard his footsteps in the corridor, and I knew he was coming back. So I thought to myself, *He already thinks I'm strange. If he comes in and finds me speaking this strange language without any explanation, he'll think me stranger still.* I decided I would explain to him what had happened.

I really don't know how I expected to explain something I didn't understand myself, but when I started to talk to him, I couldn't speak in English, so I explained in the unknown language. Sure enough, he thought I was stranger still! Fortunately, he was an agnostic. His attitude was that everybody has a right to do his own thing, and "if that's his thing, let him do it," which was pretty tolerant!

RECEIVING THE HOLY SPIRIT

I want to explain to you now how you can, in practical terms, be baptized in the Holy Spirit as a believer. The simplest way I know to describe the process is to go back to the seventh chapter of John:

> *In the last day, that great day of the feast, Jesus stood and cried, saying, If any man thirst, let him come unto me, and drink. He that believeth on me, as the scripture hath said, out of his belly shall flow rivers of living water. (But this spake he of the Spirit, which they that believe on him*

> *should receive: for the Holy Ghost was not yet given; because that Jesus was not yet glorified.)*   (John 7:37–39 KJV)

In these verses from John, Jesus described how to receive the baptism. You can receive it if you will meet the simple requirements of the Lord in faith.

Be Thirsty

Jesus said, *"If any man thirst"* (John 7:37 KJV). The first requirement is to be thirsty—in other words, to feel you need more of God than you presently have. You don't have to be a Bible student. You don't have to leave a church, join a church, quote Scripture, or pay tithes. The baptism in the Holy Spirit is for those who are thirsty. If you are not thirsty, it's a waste of your time to seek it. But you don't have to be a theologian or expert in Scripture or very spiritual. You just have to know you need more of God than you have.

One of the things I got familiar with when I was a soldier in the desert was thirst, because we were habitually short of water and it was hot and dusty. I discovered that when you are thirsty, you want only one thing, and that is to drink. You're not interested in food, you're not interested in pleasure, and you're not interested in sleep; you want to drink. That's what it is to be thirsty.

Come to Jesus

Second, Jesus said, *"Come unto me"* (John 7:37 KJV). That is very simple. There is only one Baptizer in the Holy Spirit, and it is the Lord Jesus Christ. That is His distinctive ministry. *"This is He who baptizes with the Holy Spirit"* (John 1:33). If you want the baptism, you have to come to the Baptizer. But Jesus also said, *"The one who comes to Me I will by no means cast out"* (John 6:37). So if you come, He will receive you.

Drink

Third, Jesus said, *"And drink"* (John 7:37 KJV). This is where people have trouble. "Drink" means that by a voluntary act, you receive the Spirit within you. There is a saying, "You can lead a horse to water, but you can't make it drink." Drinking only happens of a person's own volition. No one else can drink for you. You also cannot drink with your mouth closed. No one has ever received the baptism of the Holy Spirit with his mouth closed. You have to open your mouth and drink

Holy Spirit

There are three things you have to do to receive the Holy Spirit baptism: be thirsty, come to Jesus, and drink.

in—not visible water, but the Spirit of God. You say, "It looks silly." Well, who cares what it looks like? If you do care, come back when you don't. I have never yet seen a person do that without receiving the Holy Spirit.

Those are the three steps: be thirsty, come to Jesus, and drink. When you do your part, God does His. Jesus said, in essence, "When you take a drink of living water inside you, it becomes rivers." Isn't that a remarkable transformation? A person who was just a thirsty man becomes a channel of rivers of water. *"Out of his belly shall flow rivers of living water"* (John 7:38 KJV).

Holy Spirit

Once dry and thirsty, the Spirit-baptized person becomes a channel of rivers of living water for others.

When I was baptized in the Holy Spirit, there was one thing I was very conscious of; it was the fact that it started in my belly. I could put my hand exactly where it began. And I thought at the time that the belly was a sort of secular thing and was not the place for anything spiritual to begin. But Jesus said, *"Out of his belly..."* (John 7:37 KJV). Out of the innermost part of your body, somewhere inside you, will come rivers of living water. I believe there is a special area of your body created by God for the specific purpose of being the temple of the Holy Spirit. Out of that area will flow the rivers of living water.

This is the outflow. Again, *"Out of the abundance of the heart the mouth speaks"* (Matthew 12:34). The disciples were all filled with the Holy Spirit, and they began to speak. This was a supernatural infilling and a supernatural outflow. They spoke languages they didn't know.

When you come to this point, I know from experience that you may encounter two problems. First, you may tend to say, "Well, I want God to do it all." That is not scriptural. The disciples did the speaking; the Holy Spirit gave the language. The Holy Spirit will not do the speaking for you. If you wait for that, you will wait forever.

> *Holy Spirit*
>
> The disciples did the speaking; the Holy Spirit gave the language.

I met one man in a Pentecostal church who had waited for twenty-five years for the baptism. I said to him, "If you will begin to speak, the Holy Spirit will give you the words." But he replied, "Oh, no. I want God to do it all." "Well," I told him, "you want something that God doesn't want. God wants you to do your part, and He'll do His. But God will not do your part for you."

Maybe you have been conditioned to believe that this is so powerful and supernatural that you do nothing until it explodes and you can't help it. That's not right. When you speak, the Holy Spirit, who is a gentleman and doesn't force or compel you, will give you the words.

It's not a matter of feeling; it's a matter of faith in the Word of God.

The second problem comes after you start to speak in tongues. This doesn't happen to everybody, but it happens to perhaps more than half the people. There is a little inaudible voice somewhere that says, "That's not real. You're doing it yourself." When this happens, the way to respond is to say, "You're quite right, Satan, and I know it's you who is talking. I *am* doing the speaking, but the Holy Spirit is giving me the words."

Then there is one more thing Satan may say: "Those words sound very silly. How do you know you have the right thing?" Don't answer him with, "Because I feel terrific," because tomorrow morning you may feel less than terrific, and then you may wonder whether you really received the right thing. The answer to whether you have the right thing is this: Jesus promised that if you ask the Father for the Holy Spirit, He will not give you anything else.

> *What man is there among you who, if his son asks for bread, will give him a stone? Or if he asks for a fish, will he give him a serpent? If you then, being evil, know how to give good gifts to your children, how much more will your Father who is in heaven give good things to those who ask Him!* (Matthew 7:9–11)

> *If you then, being evil, know how to give good gifts to your children, how much more will your heavenly Father give the Holy Spirit to those who ask Him!*
> (Luke 11:13)

If you come to God the Father through Jesus Christ the Son and ask for the Holy Spirit, you will never receive the wrong thing. So your guarantee is not how you feel. Your guarantee is what God has said. It's not a matter of feeling; it's a matter of faith in the Word of God.

Part Two:

Living in the Fullness of *the Spirit*

Chapter 6

BEING LED BY

the Spirit

BEING LED BY THE SPIRIT

*I*n the last chapter, I mentioned five ministries of the Holy Spirit: Teacher, Remembrancer, Guide, Revelator, and Administrator. In this chapter, I want to focus on the particular ministry of the Holy Spirit as Guide.

Let's begin by looking at John 16:13 again: *"However, when He, the Spirit of truth, has come, He will guide you into all truth."* This is a clear statement from Scripture that the Holy Spirit comes to be our Guide. When we are baptized in the Holy Spirit, we must learn to be led by the Spirit and to bear the fruit of the Spirit by living in the grace Christ has provided for us.

CHRISTIAN MATURITY MEANS BEING REGULARLY LED BY THE SPIRIT

In Romans 8:14, a very significant verse, Paul spoke about how we can be fulfilled and complete Christians. *"For as many as are led by the Spirit of God, these are sons of God."* The verb tense here is the continuing present tense. In other words, as many as are *regularly* led by the Spirit of God, these are sons of God. The word *"sons"* speaks of maturity. It is not the word for a little baby but for a grown-up son. Of course, in order to become God's children, we have to be born again of the Spirit of God. Jesus spoke about that very clearly in John 3. But once we have been born again, in order to grow up and become mature and complete, we need to be consistently led by the Holy Spirit.

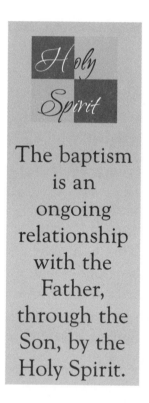

The baptism is an ongoing relationship with the Father, through the Son, by the Holy Spirit.

The sad truth is that many Christians who have been born again and even baptized in the Holy Spirit have never really gone on to be led by the Spirit. Consequently, they don't achieve maturity, and they don't become the kind of complete Christians God intends. In fact, some of the people who talk most about the Holy Spirit know least about being led by Him. I have been a Pentecostal for more than fifty years. I thank God for Pentecostals; I owe my salvation to them. But the people who say, "I was baptized in the

Holy Spirit in 1986 and I spoke in tongues, and that's it," are probably far out of touch with the Holy Spirit today. The baptism is not a onetime experience; it is an ongoing relationship with the Father, through the Son, by the Holy Spirit.

UNDERSTANDING LAW VERSUS GRACE

One reason Christians don't achieve maturity is that they have never truly understood what it means to receive the righteousness of Christ. They find it difficult to allow the Holy Spirit to be their Guide because they are relying on another method to find their way.

The Bible reveals two alternative ways to achieve righteousness with God. The distinction between the two is extremely important, and is a major theme of the New Testament; yet according to my observation, many believers pay very little attention to this particular question. These two ways are *law* and *grace*. The Bible explains very clearly that they are mutually exclusive. If you seek to achieve righteousness by the law, you

> *Holy Spirit*
>
> Our ability to be led by the Spirit depends on our understanding of law versus grace.

cannot achieve it by grace. On the other hand, if you seek to achieve righteousness by grace, then you cannot do it by keeping the law.

This truth is tremendously important because, though I may be just speaking about a limited area of the Christian church I'm familiar with, I see most Christians trying to live partly by law and partly by grace. The truth of the matter is—they don't really understand either. Yet an understanding of both is vital to learning how to be led by the Spirit.

The Nature of the Law

Law is a set of rules you have to keep. And if you keep all the rules, all the time, then you are made righteous. Grace, on the other hand, is something we cannot earn or achieve by working for it. If you are working for anything or seeking to earn it, it is not grace. Grace is received from God in one way. Ephesians 2:8 says, *"For by grace you have been saved through faith, and that not of yourselves; it is the gift of God."* Grace comes only through faith, and the result is righteousness.

Therefore, if you want to achieve righteousness, if you want to come into the maturity of God, you have to decide whether you are going to do it by law or by grace. If you follow the advice of the Bible, you won't try to do it by law, because the

Bible says no one will ever achieve righteousness with God by keeping the law.

To understand why, let's look at some of the requirements of the law. The basic principle you have to understand is this: To be righteous by keeping the law, you have to keep the *whole law, all the time.* It's not enough to keep the whole law some of the time, or some of the law all the time. If you are not continually keeping the whole law, it cannot make you righteous.

Paul explained this concept in his epistle to the Galatians. *"For as many as are of the works of the law are under the curse; for it is written, 'Cursed is everyone who does not continue in all things which are written in the book of the law, to do them'"* (Galatians 3:10). Similarly, James wrote,

> *For whoever shall keep the whole law, and yet stumble* [fail] *in one point, he is guilty of all. For He who said, "Do not commit adultery," also said, "Do not murder." Now if you do not commit adultery, but*

Holy Spirit

Many Christians try to live partly by law and partly by grace because they don't understand either one.

you do murder, you have become a trans-
gressor of the law. (James 2:10–11)

So if you want to receive the blessing and avoid the curse, you have to continue to do all things in the law all the time. You cannot single out the commandments you think are important and say, "I'll keep these, and the others I won't." You have to keep every commandment or the law is of no benefit to you *as a means of achieving righteousness.*

The Bible says that nobody ever succeeds at keeping the whole law. This fact is very clearly stated in many passages. Let's look at two of them.

Romans 3:20 says, *"Therefore by the deeds of the law* [the keeping of the law] *no flesh will be justified in His sight, for by the law is the knowledge of sin."* Paul was saying that no human being will ever achieve righteousness in God's sight by keeping a law.

You may argue, "Then why did God give the law of Moses?" The law was never actually given to make anybody righteous. One of its purposes was to show us we need to be saved. A second purpose was to show us we cannot save ourselves.

For when we were in the flesh [when we were controlled by our fleshly nature], *the sinful passions which were aroused by*

> *the law were at work in our members to*
> *bear fruit to death.* (Romans 7:5)

That's an astonishing statement. It says that the law aroused the passions of sin. This is what Paul was referring to when he said, *"The strength of sin is the law"* (1 Corinthians 15:56). The law did not stop us from sinning; it stirred up sin in us. When I was confirmed in the Anglican church at the age of fifteen, I realized for the first time that I needed to be a lot better than I was. So I learned all the questions, memorized all the answers, and said, "Now that I'm confirmed, I'm going to be better." And I was quite sincere. The problem was, the harder I tried to be good, the quicker I became bad. I was not nearly so bad until I tried to be good because I stirred up something in me. I didn't know what it was at the time, but it was what Paul called the old man, the rebel, the flesh. It is when you really try to do the right thing in your own strength that you realize you cannot do it. The harder you try, the less you succeed.

Holy Spirit

People erroneously think it will be all right if they keep most of the law some of the time.

113

A third purpose of the law was to foreshow and predict the Savior who would be able to save us.

Paul illustrated the purpose of the law when he wrote, *"The law was our tutor to bring us to Christ, that we might be justified by faith"* (Galatians 3:24). The Greek word translated *"tutor"* is *paidagogos*, from which we get the word *pedagogue*. The word originally referred to a senior slave in the household of a wealthy man, who was given charge over the children in their early years. He had two jobs. First, he was to teach the children the elements of education (such as the letters of the alphabet, obedience, and right and wrong). Then, when the children got beyond that stage, his job was to lead them through the streets and deliver them to the real teacher at the real school.

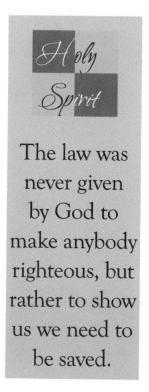

The law was never given by God to make anybody righteous, but rather to show us we need to be saved.

Thus, the law teaches us the basic elements of righteousness. However, it also leads us to the school where we can learn the real lesson, which is Christ. This is a very vivid and clarifying analogy.

In Galatians 2:16, Paul said, *"**Knowing** that a man is not justified by the works of the law"* (emphasis added). The question is, dear friends, do you truly *know* that...

> *a man is not justified by the works of the law but by faith in Jesus Christ, even we have believed in Christ Jesus, that we may be justified by faith in Christ and not by the works of the law; for by the works of the law no flesh shall be justified.*
>
> (Galatians 2:16)

We have believed in Christ so that we might be made righteous in Christ by faith, not by keeping the works of the law. Going back to the third chapter of Galatians, Paul said, *"That no one is justified by the law in the sight of God is evident, for 'the just shall live by faith'"* (Galatians 3:11). The alternative to living by the law is living by faith. These are mutually exclusive methods. It is only as we live by faith that we can trust the Holy Spirit to be our Guide and allow Him to lead us.

As I mentioned earlier, my observation is that most Christians are not living by faith. They are living in a "twilight" existence, halfway between law on the one hand and grace on the other, and they usually get the worst of both worlds. Yet the reality is—we have escaped from the dominion of the law through the death of Jesus and are now free to be led by the Spirit. Paul wrote,

Therefore, my brethren, you also have become dead to the law through the body of Christ, that you may be married to another; to Him who was raised from the dead, that we should bear fruit to God.

(Romans 7:4)

Paul was saying that when you come under the law, it's like a marriage contract by which you're joined to your fleshly nature. No matter how you try to keep the law, you don't succeed because the rebel in you won't do the right thing. But the good news is that when Jesus died on the cross, our fleshly nature was put to death in Him. *"Our old man was crucified with Him,"* Paul wrote, *"that the body of sin might be done away with, that we should no longer be slaves of sin. For he who has died has been freed from sin"* (Romans 6:6–7).

But now we have been delivered from the law, having died to what we were held by [our fleshly nature], *so that we should serve in the newness of the Spirit and not in the oldness of the letter.* (Romans 7:6)

As part of the Word of God, the law endures forever; God's Word will never pass away. But *as a means of righteousness*, Christ ended the law. *"For Christ is the end of the law for righteousness to everyone who believes"* (Romans 10:4).

Now that the flesh has been put to death, or executed, Paul said we're free for a different kind of union, a union with the resurrected Christ through the Spirit. *"That you may be married to another; to Him who was raised from the dead"* (Romans 7:4).

When we were married to the flesh, we brought forth the offspring of the flesh. But now that we are united to the resurrected Christ by the Holy Spirit, we bring forth the fruit of His righteousness, the fruit of the Spirit. In this sense it's not what we try to *do*, but it's what we're *united with* that determines the way we live. This is really the essence of the Christian message. As long as you are just trying to be good and to do the right thing, you haven't grasped the message. But when you are united with Christ, and live in that unity, then you can be led by the Spirit.

> *Holy Spirit*
>
> The good news is that we have escaped from the dominion of the law through the death of Jesus.

The Nature of Grace

Only after we realize that we are incurably sick with this disease of sin will we really want the remedy. Basically, you have to come to this point if you are really going to accept God's way of righteousness, which is grace, not law.

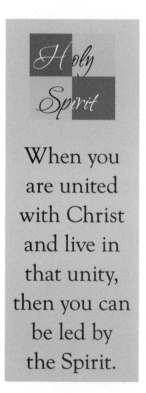

When you are united with Christ and live in that unity, then you can be led by the Spirit.

Grace is God's goodness that we don't deserve. Religious people find it hard to receive the grace of God because their thinking is, "I've got to do something to earn it." When I got saved, I ceased to be religious, so I just plunged in and got everything. I was saved, baptized in the Holy Spirit, and received gifts of the Holy Spirit within a week. Yet another soldier who went with me to the same meeting was a very earnest religious type, and it took him weeks to get what I got in a few days because he kept trying to earn it. He thought he had to be good enough to receive it.

I have talked with scores of people who don't receive the baptism in the Holy Spirit because they think they have to be good enough to earn it. You will never be good enough to earn the baptism. Nothing you can do will ever make you good enough for God the third Person to come and dwell in your physical body. You must truly understand that grace cannot be earned. We are talking about something that, if God had not chosen to do it, it would have never happened. We will never understand the grace of God, but we *can* receive it.

LIVING BY LAW OR GRACE

The crux of our discussion is this: you have to choose to live either by law or grace; you cannot have it both ways. Paul was speaking to people who had received the grace of God when he said, *"For sin shall not have dominion over you, for you are not under law but under grace"* (Romans 6:14). There is a lot of correlation between Romans and Galatians in this matter. Galatians 5:18 says, *"But if you are led by the Spirit, you are not under the law."* Notice that law and grace are mutually exclusive. If you are under law, you are not under grace. If you are under grace, you are not under law.

Paul said sin will not have dominion over you because you are not under the law. What is the implication? If you *are* under the law, sin *will* have dominion over you. Do you see that? This is a very important verse. It teaches us two things. First, if we try to achieve righteousness by law, sin will have dominion over us. Second, if we want to achieve righteousness by grace, we cannot achieve it by law.

Let's look again at Romans 8:14, which we discussed at the beginning of the chapter: *"For as many as are led by the Spirit of God, these are sons of God."* How do we live as sons of God? By keeping a set of rules? No. By being led by the Holy Spirit. That is the only way we can live as God's mature, grown-up children.

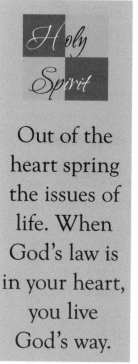

Out of the heart spring the issues of life. When God's law is in your heart, you live God's way.

For most professing Christians, law or a set of rules is like a crutch. They limp around, supporting themselves with it. God says, "Throw the crutch away and trust Me." They ask themselves, "But what will I do without my crutch?" I have discovered that it frightens people to trust God's grace and to really commit themselves to it.

In his second letter to the Corinthian church, Paul wrote to the believers there,

> *You are an epistle of Christ, ministered by us, written not with ink but by the Spirit of*

*the living God, not on tablets of stone but
on tablets of flesh, that is, of the heart.*
(2 Corinthians 3:3)

Proverbs 4:23 says, *"Keep your heart with
all diligence, for out of it spring the issues of life."*
When God's law is in your heart, you live God's
way.

The issue of grace versus law is real to me
because I have struggled through it. I have worked
hard to be more religious, and I have felt so frus-
trated that I didn't know what to do. But I have
learned this is part of the process that makes
a Christian and teaches us to rely on the Holy
Spirit. I therefore want to relate two parables, in
order to make what it means to be led by the Holy
Spirit more vivid to you.

TWO PARABLES OF LAW AND GRACE

Rebekah and Abraham's Servant

In an earlier chapter, we talked briefly about
how Abraham sent his servant to find a bride for
his son Isaac among his relatives in Mesopota-
mia. This was a historical event, but it is also a
parable for us. Again, Abraham is a type of God
the Father; Isaac is a type of Jesus Christ, the
only Son; and Rebekah, the chosen bride, is a
type of the church. The other main character is

Abraham's servant or steward, who is a type of the Holy Spirit.

The steward goes out taking ten camels with all sorts of equipment and laden with gifts because he is going to choose a bride. In the Middle East, whenever you make a significant choice and build a relationship, you always give a gift. And if you receive such a gift, you have received the person. If you refuse the gift, you have refused the person. The giving of the gift is an absolutely critical moment.

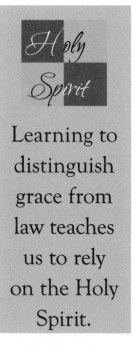

Holy Spirit

Learning to distinguish grace from law teaches us to rely on the Holy Spirit.

I have lived in the Middle East, and let me tell you—camels can carry a lot. They are able to carry an immense amount of luggage. And the steward had *ten* camels. He arrived in the area of Abraham's homeland, stopped at a well, and prayed to God, saying,

> *Behold, here I stand by the well of water, and the daughters of the men of the city are coming out to draw water. Now let it be that the young woman to whom I say,*

"Please let down your pitcher that I may drink," and she says, "Drink, and I will also give your camels a drink"; let her be the one You have appointed for Your servant Isaac. And by this I will know that You have shown kindness to my master.
(Genesis 24:13–14)

We should bear in mind that a camel can drink forty gallons of water. So, the amount you would need for ten camels is about four hundred gallons of water!

Well, along came Rebekah, and the steward said, "Please give me a drink of water." And she said, "Certainly. And I'll draw for your camels." Let me tell you, that is an example of faith with works! The steward said to himself, *This is the girl.* He pulled out beautiful jewelry and gave it to her. The moment she wore the jewelry, it marked her out as the appointed bride. What would have happened if she had refused the jewelry? She never would have become the bride. (See verses 15–22.)

If you refuse the gift, then you are refusing the One who gives the gift.

123

When Abraham's servant was ready to return home, Rebekah's family asked her,

> *"Will you go with this man?" And she said, "I will go."...Then Rebekah and her maids arose, and they rode on the camels and followed the man.*
>
> (Genesis 24:58, 61)

I want to point out to you that Rebekah never had a map. She'd never been where she was going. She had never seen the man she was to marry, and she had never seen his father. She only had one source of information, the steward. He was her guide, and she trusted him to bring her to her bridegroom.

Choosing between the Map and the Guide

The second parable concerns a young man who needs to find the way to a distant destination over country that he has never traveled before. He has two options. He can have a map or he can have a personal guide. The map is the law. It is perfect. Every detail is exactly right. Every single item in the geography is correctly marked. The personal guide is the Holy Spirit.

This young man has just graduated from the university. He's strong, clever, and pretty self-reliant. God asks him, "What do you want, the

map or the guide?" He says, "I'm good at reading maps, so I'll take the map." He sets off down
the road, knowing the right direction to go. The
sun is shining, the birds are singing, and he feels
happy. He says, "This is a piece of cake."

About three days later, he's in the middle
of a jungle, it's midnight, it's
raining hard, and he's on the
edge of a precipice. He does
not know whether he is facing north, south, east, or west.
Then a gentle voice says to
him, "Can I help you?" And he
says, "Oh, Holy Spirit! I need
you!" The Holy Spirit says,
"Give me your hand, and I'll
get you out of this." A little
while later, they are out on the
road again and walking along
side by side.

> ## *Holy Spirit*
>
> The Holy
> Spirit knows
> the way
> because He
> is the One
> who charted
> the map.

Then it occurs to the young
man, *I was pretty silly to get so
panicky just about being in that
jungle. I could have made it on my own.* So he
turns around and says, "I can make it by myself."
He doesn't see the Guide any longer, so off he sets.
About two days later, he is in the middle of a bog,
and every step he takes, he sinks a little deeper.

He does not know what to do, but he thinks to himself, *I can't ask for help again. The last time I received it, I didn't do the right thing.* But then the Holy Spirit says, "Let Me help you." And out they come onto the road again, and they set off.

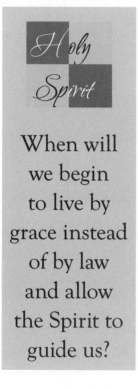

Holy Spirit

When will we begin to live by grace instead of by law and allow the Spirit to guide us?

They are making fine progress, and then the young man thinks, *I've still got the map.* He pulls out the map and says to the Holy Spirit, "Maybe You'd like the map." The Holy Spirit answers, "Thanks, but I know the way. I don't need the map. As a matter of fact, I made the map."

My question to you and me is this: How many times will we go back to trusting in our own wisdom or cleverness and snubbing the Holy Spirit? When will we begin to live by grace and not by law and allow the Spirit to guide us?

Rebekah and the young man in these two parables are symbolic of us. We can make it to our destination if we trust the Holy Spirit, our Guide. The Holy Spirit is our source of information. He is the Administrator of our eternal inheritance. He will tell us what to expect, and He will give us everything we need.

Chapter 7

YIELDING TO THE
Holy Spirit

YIELDING TO THE HOLY SPIRIT

*A*long with understanding the difference between living by law and living by grace, we need to fully comprehend the new nature we have been given in Christ. In this way, we can live and walk in the Spirit as God intends.

Many people who have been baptized in the Holy Spirit, and who say that the Holy Spirit dwells in them, do not actually *live* in the Spirit. I know people who are baptized in the Spirit but are very obviously living according to the flesh much of the time. They can be extremely unpleasant, carnal, and lacking in faith and love and other qualities of the Spirit. If we are honest about it, we all struggle to varying degrees with this issue of flesh versus Spirit. Yet God has provided the solution for us.

OUR REBELLIOUS NATURE WAS EXECUTED

We learned in the last chapter that the law incites our fleshly nature and that we need to live in grace. Yet some of us retain the mind-set that we are still "married" to the fleshly nature and therefore find it difficult to live in the fullness of the Spirit.

We know that every one of us is born with a rebellious nature, or the *"old man"* (Romans 6:6), and this nature is the root of our problems. On the cross, Jesus, by the Father's will, made Himself one with that rebellious nature, and the old man was executed in Him. God has no program of rehabilitation for the old man. He doesn't send him to church or Sunday school. He doesn't teach him Scripture or make him religious. God's program is summed up in one simple word: *execution.* He can do nothing with the old man except to kill him. Our rebellious nature was executed when Christ died on the cross so that it should no longer have the power to dominate and control us.

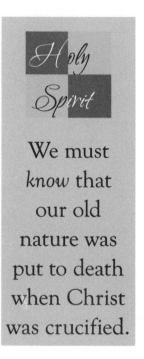

We must *know* that our old nature was put to death when Christ was crucified.

This is a historical fact, but won't do us any good unless we know it and act upon it. The first requirement is to know it. I have found that it is not often taught, and Christians cannot enter into that which they don't know. So the first requirement is truly knowing what happened in respect to the old nature when Christ died on the cross: it was decisively put to death.

God forgives our past sinful acts when we come to Him in Christ, but this is only the beginning. He deals with the rebellious nature, and He brings forth a new nature in its place, which is called the new man. This is actually the nature of Jesus Christ reproduced in us by faith from the seed of the Word of God. The agent who produces the new birth is the Holy Spirit, and the Holy Spirit ministers the Christ nature in us.

In Romans, Paul said,

What shall we say then? Shall we continue in sin that grace may abound? Certainly not! How shall we who died to sin live any longer in it? (Romans 6:1–2)

Paul assumed that anybody living in the grace of God was dead to sin, so he was saying, "If you continue to live in sin, you're contradicting yourself. If you're dead to sin, you shouldn't talk about living in sin."

After Christ died on the cross, He did not raise Himself from the dead. He trusted the Father to raise Him at the appointed hour, through the Holy Spirit. If the Father had not raised Him, He would have remained dead. Likewise, we have to trust God to raise us out of the death of our sins. We cannot do it by ourselves. We are as much dependent on the Holy Spirit for this as Jesus was for the physical resurrection of His body. In fact, this is the public testimony we give when we are baptized in water: "I'm buried, and it's up to God to resurrect me. When I walk out of this watery grave, I walk out saying, 'I'm relying on the Holy Spirit as much as Jesus relied on the Holy Spirit to raise Him in newness of life.'"

> *Therefore we were buried with Him through baptism into death, that just as Christ was raised from the dead by the glory of the Father, even so we also should walk in newness of life. For if we have been united together in the likeness of His death, certainly we also shall be in the likeness of His resurrection.* (Romans 6:4–5)

Only the Holy Spirit can enable us to react appropriately to the gospel. Without the Holy Spirit, we just can't do it. But when we receive the Spirit, and live in the Spirit, then the seemingly unattainable standards in the Bible begin to become spontaneous reality.

Paul wrote, *"But ye are not in the flesh, but in the Spirit, if so be that the Spirit of God dwell in you"* (Romans 8:9 KJV). I will tell you what I believe this verse is saying to us. The Greek word translated *"if so be"* sets a condition. The same word is used in Romans 8:17: *"...if so be that we suffer with him"* (KJV). I'll give you the "Prince Bible version" of verse nine. This is the way I have worked it out: "But ye are not in the flesh, but in the Spirit, *insofar as* the Spirit of God dwells in you." Many people have the Spirit of God dwelling in some areas of their lives but not in others. Therefore, "insofar as" the Spirit of God dwells in you, you are not in the flesh, but in the Spirit.

Again, many people who are baptized in the Holy Spirit are not fully under the control of the Holy Spirit. There are some circumstances, and there are certain times (usually in church), where they are under the control of the Holy Spirit, and there are other circumstances and times where they are not. This fact hits very close to home for many of us. I don't believe in an unrealistic theology that sounds all right but doesn't

> When you live in the Spirit, the Bible's seemingly unattainable standards become reality.

work. I have discovered that the New Testament works when we understand it and apply it. So if you have received the Holy Spirit, insofar as you are yielded to the Holy Spirit and allowing Him to indwell every area of your life, in that regard you are not in the flesh, but in the Spirit.

Going back to Romans 6, Paul said,

Knowing this, that our old man was crucified with Him, that the body of sin might be done away with, that we should no longer be slaves of sin. (Romans 6:6)

*"Our old man **was** crucified with Him."* It is the simple past tense, not the perfect tense. This signifies it is a historical event that took place at a certain moment in the past. When Jesus died on the cross, our old man died in Him. It happened twenty centuries ago. Why was this done? *"That the body of sin might be done away with."* A better way of saying this might be "rendered ineffective," or "no longer able to control and dominate us" so *"that we should no longer be slaves of sin"* (Romans 6:6).

Probably 95 percent of Christians don't know their old nature was crucified. But when you know it, you can appropriate God's provision. Because our sin was dealt with in Christ on the cross, it is now possible *"that the righteous requirement of the law might be fulfilled in us who do not walk according to the flesh but according to the Spirit"* (Romans 8:4). Paul encouraged us,

> *Likewise* [in precisely the same way] *you also, reckon yourselves to be dead indeed to sin* [not just in theory, but in fact], *but alive to God in Christ Jesus our Lord.*
>
> (Romans 6:11)

He was saying, "Exactly as Christ died on the cross, was buried, and rose again from the dead, never to die again but to live forever unto God, consider yourself to have truly died unto sin and to have come alive to God." It is impossible to live in the fullness of life in the Holy Spirit that Paul described in the eighth chapter of Romans until you have acquired the truth of the sixth chapter of Romans. The old rebellious Adamic nature cannot live according to the Spirit. At the beginning of Romans 8, Paul clearly emphasized this:

> *For those who live according to the flesh set their minds on the things of the flesh, but those who live according to the Spirit, the things of the Spirit. For to be carnally minded* [to have the mind of the flesh— the reactions, reasoning, thinking, and motivations of the flesh] *is death, but to be spiritually minded* [to think the way the

Spirit thinks] *is life and peace. Because the carnal mind is enmity against God; for it is not subject to the law of God, nor indeed can be. So then, those who are in the flesh cannot please God.*

(Romans 8:5–8)

It is *impossible* for the old nature to please God. Therefore, it must first be dealt with before we can live and please God. And God's provision for the old Adamic nature is the cross and the death of Jesus. We must come to truly understand this.

REFUSE TO ACCEPT THE DOMINION OF SIN OVER YOU

Returning to Romans 6, we come to the results of reckoning ourselves dead to sin:

Therefore do not let sin reign in your mortal body, that you should obey it in its lusts. And do not present your members as instruments of unrighteousness to sin, but present yourselves to God as being alive from the dead, and your members as instruments of righteousness to God.

(Romans 6:12–13)

Refuse any longer to accept the dominion of sin over you and the members of your physical body, but instead yield yourself—your will and your members—to God the Holy Spirit. This leads to the assurance,

> *For sin shall not have dominion over you....* (Romans 6:14)

Do you believe that? If you do not believe it, you will not experience it. If you believe that you are going to continue sinning, you will continue sinning, for sure. Because it is by faith. *"Sin shall not have dominion over you."* You have to believe it. If you do not believe it, it will not happen. Notice how the second half of the verse goes with the first half:

> *...for you are not under law but under grace.* (verse 14)

If you are going to walk in the Spirit, you cannot walk in the flesh. If you walk in the flesh, you cannot be led by the Spirit. There is a total incompatibility. Every person must come to the place of a firm personal decision: Where do I belong? In the flesh or in the Spirit?

Yielding to the Spirit and being led by Him is the way of escape from continuing in the slavery of sin. Let me put it this way: what is the good of having your past sinful acts forgiven if you are still controlled by the rebellious nature? All you do is go out and commit the same sinful acts again. But we are no longer living in the old carnal nature; we have a new nature supplied by the Holy Spirit.

> *Therefore, brethren, we are debtors; not to the flesh, to live according to the flesh.* [We don't owe the flesh anything. We never got anything good out of it, so let's stop cultivating it and instead cultivate the new nature.] *For if you* [Spirit-baptized believers] *live according to the flesh you will die.* (Romans 8:12–13)

Our problem is that we read the epistles as if they were written to unbelievers. When Paul said, *"Do not be deceived, God is not mocked; for whatever a man sows, that he will also reap"* (Galatians 6:7), he was not talking to unbelievers but believers. In Galatians 6:8, Paul wrote, *"For he who sows to his flesh will of the flesh reap corruption."* In Romans 8:13, he said, *"If you live according to the flesh you will die."* If you voluntarily and deliberately go back into the old, unregenerate, rebellious nature, you will die.

> *But if by the Spirit* [with the help of the Holy Spirit] *you put to death the deeds of the body, you will live.* (Romans 8:13)

The Holy Spirit will help you if you set your will to it. But if you don't set your will to it, the Holy Spirit won't do it for you.

In Latin, the word for character is the plural of the word for habit. That is very illuminating. Your character is the sum total of your habits, and your habits are produced by the sum total of your decisions. Every time you make a right decision, you are strengthening a right habit. Every time you strengthen a right habit, you are building a right character. Every time you make a wrong decision, you are building a wrong habit, and out of that wrong habit, you are building a wrong character.

So you have to build habits by decision. Every time you make a decision to do the wrong thing, you become more and more the slave of sin; every time you make a decision to do the right thing, you become more and more the slave of righteousness.

Do you not know that to whom you present yourselves slaves to obey, you are that

> Every time you make the right decision, you strengthen a right habit and build a right character.

> *one's slaves whom you obey, whether of sin*
> *leading to death, or of obedience leading*
> *to righteousness?* (Romans 6:16)

When you commit a sinful act, you are yielding to sin; if you yield to sin, you become the slave of sin and cannot help sinning. If you yield to righteousness, however, you become the slave of righteousness, and you do what is righteous. You must be in one category or the other. Joshua 24:15 says it as plain as it can ever be said: *"Choose for yourselves this day whom you will serve."* The choice is not whether you will serve, it is *whom*. You are going to serve someone, and you have two options: God or the devil; righteousness or sin.

> *For as many as are* [regularly] *led by the*
> *Spirit of God, these are sons of God.*
> (Romans 8:14)

In order to *become* a child of God, you must be born again. To *receive the power* to be an effective witness, you must be baptized in the Holy Spirit. But to *live* as a son of God, you must be daily led by the Holy Spirit.

Some teach that you have to be super-spiritual first, and one day you will emerge as a son of God. But this idea is in direct conflict with Romans 8:14, which says all who are regularly led by the Holy

Spirit are the sons of God. As I wrote in an earlier chapter, the word here isn't *children* but *"sons."* A maturity is implied. Too many people have the attitude, "When I'm perfect, the Holy Spirit will come in." That essentially used to be Pentecostal teaching. It is rather like some young people attending a university and the professors coming in and saying to them, "When you graduate, we'll start to teach you." Well, when you graduate, you don't need the professors. You need the professors *to* graduate. Likewise, when do you need the Holy Spirit? Right now, in order to become mature. The Holy Spirit does not come to you because you are perfect; He comes to you because you need Him.

> *I speak in human terms because of the weakness of your flesh. For just as you presented your members as slaves of uncleanness, and of lawlessness leading to more lawlessness, so now present your members as slaves of righteousness for holiness. For when you were slaves of sin, you were free in regard to righteousness.* [Righteousness had no control over you.] *What fruit did you have then in the things of which you are now ashamed? For the end of those things is death.* [Be very clear about that!] *But now having been set free from sin, and having become*

> *slaves of God, you have your fruit to holi-*
> *ness, and the end, everlasting life.*
> (Romans 6:19–22)

Romans 6 has taught us that the way to become a slave of righteousness is to practice the following:

- *Know that your old nature was crucified in Christ.* (See Romans 6:6.) If you don't know this, you can't enjoy the life of the Spirit. The great enemy is ignorance. If you do not know what the Scripture teaches, if you do not know what Christ has done for you, and if you do not know the provision God has made for you, then you cannot enter into their fullness.

- *Reckon yourself dead to sin.* (See Romans 6:11.) You have to believe it. You have to say, "That's what God says, and I consider it true in me." Reckoning by faith means that God says it and I believe it.

- *Confess, or make public, your faith.* (See Romans 6:3–4.) You cannot be a secret believer in Jesus. Water baptism is the outward, appointed act of confession of your position in Christ. When are you buried? When you are dead. When are you no longer buried? When you are resurrected; when you are alive once more.

- *Do not yield to sin.* (See Romans 6:12–13.) One of the essentials of Spirit-filled living is learning how to say *no* and mean it. The devil knows when you mean it and when you don't. The book of Proverbs says, *"My son, if sinners entice you, do not consent"* (Proverbs 1:10). In plain language, say, "No." You have to be able to say no to many choices and people.

- *Yield to God.* (See Romans 6:13.) Daily, regularly, you have to yield to the Holy Spirit and be led by Him.

Jesus gave us the most beautiful invitation, followed by a tremendous challenge, in regard to yielding to righteousness:

> *Come to Me, all you who labor and are heavy laden, and I will give you rest. Take My yoke upon you and learn from Me, for I am gentle and lowly in heart, and you will find rest for your souls. For My yoke is easy and My burden is light.*
>
> (Matthew 11:28–30)

This passage suggests a process by which we yield to the Lord and learn His ways. First, we lay down our heavy burdens and have rest. Some people think that is all there is to it, but there is more. We must become disciples by taking Christ's yoke and learning from Him. Next, we follow Jesus' example of being gentle and lowly in heart, because God teaches the gentle and lowly but resists the proud. Then and only then will we find true rest—when we have taken the yoke of Jesus and become gentle, lowly, and teachable. *"For My yoke is easy and My burden is light."*

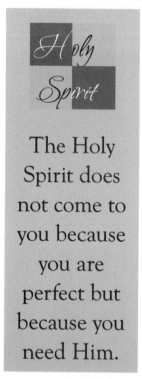

The Holy Spirit does not come to you because you are perfect but because you need Him.

Salvation does not mean getting rid of every yoke. It is an exchange of yokes. You put off the devil's yoke, but you put on the Lord's. Don't try to live without a yoke, because you can't do it. We can't say, "I don't want to serve the devil, but I don't intend to serve God," because we will end up serving the devil twice as much as before.

NOT STRUGGLING BUT UNION

I believe this is the simple scriptural pattern for passing from death to life, for passing out of the dominion of the old nature and the law, and into newness of life in Christ and in the Spirit. We must yield to the Holy Spirit and righteousness.

God's way of righteousness and holiness, therefore, is not struggling but *yielding*. You must come to the end of your efforts and say, "Holy Spirit, take over. I can't handle this situation, but You can." It doesn't mean you don't need willpower. It means you have to use your willpower differently; you have to use it *not* to try to do it yourself.

I am a very independent, strong-minded person. My natural instinct is to think of a solution any time I have a problem. It has taken me years to come to the place where I no longer do that. Now, I say, "Lord, what is Your solution?" Often, it is very different from anything I ever would have thought of. The Christian life is not a life of struggle; it is a life of yielding to the Holy Spirit within us. Then it is not effort but *union*.

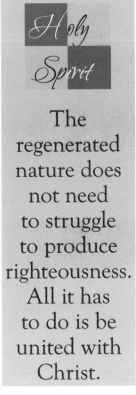

The regenerated nature does not need to struggle to produce righteousness. All it has to do is be united with Christ.

We talked about this concept of union in the previous chapter. The question is, What are you married to? If you are married to your fleshly nature, you will bring forth the works of the flesh. You can disagree with this fact as much as you like, but it is a biological law. No matter how much the old nature struggles, it still produces sin. However, if, by the Holy Spirit, you are united with the resurrected Christ, through that union you will bring forth the fruit of the Spirit. The union of the regenerated spirit with the resurrected Christ by the Holy Spirit produces the fruits of righteousness. The regenerated nature does not need to strive to produce righteousness. All it has to do is be united with Christ. So this is a life of yielding, not struggling; union, not effort.

The analogy of the vine and the branches in John 15 helps us to better understand this life. Jesus said to His disciples,

> *I am the true vine, and My Father is the vinedresser.* (John 15:1)

Vines are fruit-bearing plants that need very careful pruning. If you fail to prune a vine at the right time of year, in the right way, it ceases to bring forth grapes. Jesus was therefore saying, "I am the vine, and My Father is the one who does the pruning." He went on to say,

> *Abide in Me, and I in you. As the branch cannot bear fruit of itself, unless it abides in the vine, neither can you, unless you abide in Me. I am the vine, you are the*

branches. He who abides in Me, and I in him, bears much fruit; for without Me you can do nothing. (John 15:4–5)

A branch does not go through a lot of effort to bear grapes. It doesn't make resolutions and say, "I'm going to bring forth fruit." Instead, it is united to the trunk of the vine. The same life that is in the trunk flows through the branches in the sap, and the life in the branches brings forth the appropriate kind of fruit. Jesus said, *"'I am the vine, you are the branches.'* If you will remain related to Me, in Me, joined to Me, you'll bring forth much fruit."

Jesus also gave us a warning that is very important. He said we have to expect to be pruned. *"Every branch that bears fruit He* [the Father] *prunes, that it may bear more fruit"* (John 15:2). Some Christians have problems because they are not bearing much fruit. They struggle with situations that are the results of their bad decisions or actions. Other Christians, however, experience problems because they *are* bearing fruit. These problems are really spiritual pruning. If you have ever seen a vine pruned, the process is ruthless. The branches are cut right back to the stem. You would think the vine was never going to bear fruit again. But the next year it is more fruitful than ever.

Note that a beautiful picture of the three persons of the Godhead emerges in this Scripture passage about the vine and the branches. The Father is the vinedresser, Jesus is the vine, and the Holy Spirit is the sap that flows up through the vine and into the branches. This life of the Spirit is what brings forth fruit. Not the fruit of our best efforts, and not the fruit of religion, but the fruit of the Spirit.

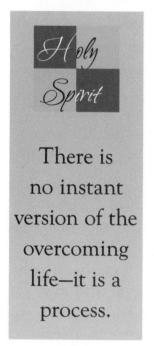

There is no instant version of the overcoming life—it is a process.

When the Father is pruning us, we must not give up in the midst of the process. We shouldn't say, "Why is this happening to me? I've sincerely tried to serve the Lord. I'm really doing my best, and I've done this, this, and this." We have borne fruit, and now we are going to be purged. During these times, we need to breathe a sigh of relief and praise God. It is a good sign.

The main point I want to emphasize is that bearing the fruit of the Spirit is not an effort. All our efforts won't do it, just as no effort will produce one grape in a thousand years. Only union with the Vine will do it. Many people want the overcoming life of the Spirit, but they don't realize there is no instant version. Victorious, Spirit-filled living is arrived at by God's process.

WE YIELD, AND GOD COMPLETES THE WORK

We come now to the fact that when we are in line with the will of God, when we are walking according to His purposes, everything we experience works together for good, and He completes His purposes in us. There is a beautiful song that says, "My Father planned it all." And that really is the truth for those who are walking in harmony with the Spirit of God. Every situation, every experience, is working out God's good, eternal purposes in us. *"All things work together for good to those who love God, to those who are the called according to His purpose"* (Romans 8:28). Notice the qualification here: we must be in line with His purpose.

Paul described the Roman believers as *"beloved of God, called to be saints"* (Romans 1:7). The word *saint* simply means "holy." *"To be"* was actually added by the translators. The Greek literally says, "called holy ones." Holiness is not some kind of extra qualification that a few believers may acquire; it is expected of all believers. Paul didn't conceive of some special super class of believers who go on to a higher plane not available to the rest of us. Paul assumed all believers were going to be holy.

When you accept the gospel invitation of faith in Jesus Christ, God calls you a holy one. You are a set-apart one who is ready to yield to the Holy Spirit and righteousness. You may look at yourself and say, "Well, I really don't seem to be very holy," but remember that Paul also said God *"calls things that are not as though they were"* (Romans 4:17 NIV). God called Abraham a father of many nations before he had even one son. (See Genesis 17:4–5.) When God calls you something, it is because He is going to make you something. When God calls you holy, you are holy because He called you holy. It may take some time to work out in your life, but that is His decree for you.

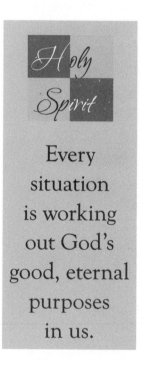

Every situation is working out God's good, eternal purposes in us.

When we received Jesus Christ, He poured out the totality of His life in the Holy Spirit upon us. He gives us what we need to live a life in the Spirit and become holy. For example, Romans 5:5 says, *"The love of God has been poured out in our hearts by the Holy Spirit who was given to us."* The

Greek perfect tense is used here, which denotes a completed action that never has to be repeated. It is vital that we understand this. *"The love of God **has been poured out** into our hearts by the Holy Spirit who **was given** to us."* In fact, once you are baptized in the Holy Spirit, you really should never pray for love again, but should draw on the inexhaustible source that you have inside you. This is the correct scriptural response. The love of God—not part of God's love but *the* love of God in its totality—has been poured out into our hearts in the gift of the Holy Spirit. All the divine love is available to us. But if we do not draw upon it, we will not experience it.

The same thing may be applied to the place of the Holy Spirit in our prayer lives. Just before Paul talked about all things working out for our good, he said,

> *Likewise the Spirit also helps in our weaknesses. For we do not know what we should pray for as we ought, but the Spirit Himself makes intercession for us with groanings which cannot be uttered. Now He who searches the hearts knows what the mind of the Spirit is, because He makes intercession for the saints according to the will of God.* (Romans 8:26–27)

I mentioned earlier that this passage deals with the fact that we all have an infirmity, a weakness. It is common to the whole human race. It is not a physical sickness; it is that we do not know how to pray as we should. I have never found anybody who disputed this statement. When I talk to people, they all acknowledge that they do not always know what to pray for; and even when they know *what* to pray for, they do not know *how* to pray for it.

What is God's answer to our weakness? The Holy Spirit. He comes to help us in our infirmity by taking over for us. When we yield to Him in prayer, He prays through us. And when He prays, it is the right prayer. It is according to the mind of God, and it will produce the results that God desires in the lives of the people for whom we are praying.

We see this clearly in our experience of the baptism in the Holy Spirit. When we speak in tongues, we know it is not our mind praying because we don't understand what is being said. We know that the Holy Spirit is supplying the prayer. All we are supplying is the mechanism, the vocal apparatus that enables the Holy Spirit to pray.

My first wife had a unique prayer life. I have never met anybody else who prayed exactly as she did. People sometimes asked her, "What's the secret of prayer?" She would say, "I just open my mouth wide and let the Holy Spirit fill it." You can do the same. Just begin in faith, and then let the Holy Spirit take over. This is how we pray the effectual prayer from the mind of God.

You cannot have a Christian prayer life in the natural. For instance, Ephesians 6:18 says, *"Praying always with all prayer and supplication in the Spirit,"* and 1 Thessalonians 5:17 says, *"Pray without ceasing."* You can't do that in your own strength and resources. But in the Spirit, you can! Paul gave us insight into how we can do this when he wrote, *"Do not quench the Spirit"* (1 Thessalonians 5:19). That is the answer. If you are not quenching the Spirit but instead living according to the Spirit, you can have a prayer meeting going on inside you twenty-four hours a day.

> When God calls you something, it is because He is going to make you something.

What I am describing is a prayer life that is not on the natural plane, but it is the will of God for us. When we accept the help of the Holy Spirit,

155

He makes it possible. This is why I have reservations about giving people a whole set of rules for prayer. Sometimes we are so busy with the rules that we leave the Holy Spirit out. We have to really be convinced of our dependence on Him.

I once used a Bible study course that included a study on prayer. It had about twenty-three questions but not one reference to the Holy Spirit. That is like having a university without a professor! The typical Christian approach to prayer is to try to do it yourself. We can't! We have to turn over control to the Holy Spirit and yield to Him because we can only truly pray according to God's will through Him.

LET THE HOLY SPIRIT LIVE THROUGH YOU

In every area of the Christian life, therefore, we are incapable in our natural ability of doing what God requires. Our natural inclinations are to live according to the flesh and to try to do things our own way. This way leads to weakness and death. God's solution is the Holy Spirit. He confines us to the impossible and then says, "Now, let the Holy Spirit do it." As we yield to Him, He will.

Chapter 8

LEARNING TO HEAR
God's Voice

LEARNING TO HEAR GOD'S VOICE

A s we saw in the parable of the young man in a previous chapter, if we don't allow the Holy Spirit to guide us, we can't hear the words of comfort, direction, and wisdom He desires to give us. I am convinced that the greatest need in our lives is to take time with God. I am sorry to say that most Christians don't give God much time—a condition for which many of us need to repent.

My wife, Ruth, and I have learned—and this is on a small scale—to take one day a week to wait upon God. We have no idea what will happen. We have no agenda; we have no prayer list. Sometimes we start by reading the Bible, and sometimes not. But at the end of the day, we tend to say to ourselves, "How did we ever get here?" We had no plan or thought of being involved in what we are in at the end of the day. The Holy Spirit has led us there.

When we learn to wait on God, He shows us blockages in our relationships with Him so that we can become free of them and love and serve Him better. Many of you are not where you ought to be with God right now. My desire is not to accuse or condemn but to help.

ACKNOWLEDGING THE HEADSHIP OF JESUS

In most of the body of Christ, something is out of place that needs to be corrected so we will take the time to wait on God and hear from Him. What is out of place? We are not acknowledging the headship of Christ in our lives.

Paul wrote in Ephesians,

> [God] *put all things under* [Jesus'] *feet, and gave Him to be head over all things to the church, which is His body, the fullness of Him who fills all in all.*
> (Ephesians 1:22–23)

Paul used an interesting choice of language here. God *put* all things under the feet of Jesus. They were subjected to Him. But He also *gave* Jesus to the church. Having Jesus as Head is a most precious and wonderful blessing for the body of Christ. And Jesus is Head over all things. Not over a few things, not over most things. Over all things.

Can you honestly say in the presence of God that Jesus is Head over everything in your life? That there is nothing that is outside His control? Nothing that is outside the expression of His determined will for you?

Later on in Ephesians, Paul wrote,

Speaking the truth in love, [we] may grow up in all things into Him who is the head; Christ; from whom the whole body, joined and knit together by what every joint supplies, according to the effective working by which every part does its share, causes growth of the body for the edifying of itself in love. (Ephesians 4:15–16)

Notice that the whole body depends on the Head. It is only through the body's relationship to the Head that the body derives nourishment and is able to grow and function effectively. If the relationship to the Head is impaired, the whole life of the body is automatically impaired.

Paul also said, *"Let no one cheat you of your reward"* (Colossians 2:18). "Let no one *disqualify* you" would better express what Paul was saying here. Don't let such a person deceive you and cheat you out of the rightful inheritance God intends you to have. This type of person takes *"delight in false humility..., vainly puffed up by his fleshly mind"* (verse 18). Such a person claims to be super-spiritual but is actually very carnal. He is puffed up in his own mind so that he does not hold *"fast to the Head, from whom all the body, nourished and knit together by joints and ligaments, grows with the increase that is from God"* (verse 19). The *New International Version* says, *"He has lost connection with the Head."*

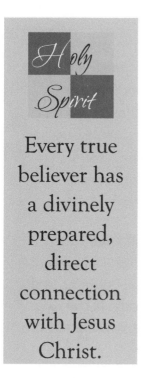

Every true believer has a divinely prepared, direct connection with Jesus Christ.

As soon as we lose connection with the Head, we are in danger of getting into error, some form of deception, some kind of false teaching, something that is out of line with the truth of God. The only condition of safety for the body collectively, and for each believer individually, is to be rightly related to the Head. Every true believer has a divinely prepared, direct connection with Jesus Christ that he must not let anyone interfere with.

Pastors are wonderful people, but they cannot take the place of Jesus. The function of a pastor is not to be your head; it is to help you cultivate your relationship with the One who is your Head. It is not to tell you the answers to all your problems; it is to show you how to find the answers for yourself from Jesus.

Some people are lazy, and they just want some human being to solve all their problems. It doesn't work that way. In addition, some leaders are despotic; they want to take control of people. I have been through all that and, thank God, I have come out of it. I have no desire to be in it again. You have to have your own personal relationship with Jesus. You have to be able to hear Him speak to you. You have to be able to be directed by Him. You have to have something inside you that tells you when He is pleased and when He is not pleased. You have to be sensitive to the Head.

FOUR FUNCTIONS OF THE HEAD

I now want to discuss four functions of our physical heads and how they relate to the headship of Jesus. I am not competent to give a lesson in anatomy, and so these are just simple, practical perspectives. As we review these four, I want you to consider your own relationship with Jesus, as well as the relationship of the church today with its Head.

It seems to me that our heads have four main functions.

- *To receive input.* Every part of the body has a right to communicate with the head, and the head receives ongoing communication from all parts of the body.

- *To make decisions.* The head decides what the body is to do.

- *To initiate an action.* The key word is *initiate* because the one who takes the initiative is the head.

- *To coordinate the activity of the members,* who carry out the decisions of the head.

The Spirit is the means by which Jesus, as the Head, communicates with the body, directs the body, controls the body, and preserves the body. So, we are not merely talking about a relationship with Jesus, but also a relationship with the Holy Spirit. Let's review some Scriptures along these lines.

Jesus said, *"When He, the Spirit of truth, has come, He will guide you into all truth"* (John 16:13). Remember that Jesus said this to His disciples when He was about to leave them, indicating, in effect, "I can't tell you everything you need to know now. But that doesn't matter, because the Spirit of truth, the Holy Spirit, is coming, and He will guide you into all truth." Jesus was saying that from that time forward, His relationship with us would be effected through the Holy Spirit.

Then He went on to say, *"For He will not speak on His own authority, but whatever He hears He will speak; and He will tell you things to come"* (John 16:13). I believe the church should have direction concerning the future—supernatural direction from the Holy Spirit. Not about everything, but for certain things we need to know.

In view of the world situation, for the church to go into the future without the Holy Spirit's guidance is to head toward disaster. We have only just glimpsed the troubles and the pressures that are coming on the whole world, and not least on the United States of America. We are going to need the Holy Spirit to warn us of what is going to happen so we won't be in the wrong place at the wrong time. One of the prayers that I pray regularly is to be always in the right place at the right time. Only the Holy Spirit can make that possible.

> *Holy Spirit*
>
> The Holy Spirit is the means by which Jesus directs His body, the church.

Then Jesus said, *"He* [the Holy Spirit] *will glorify Me"* (John 16:14). It is worth noting again, in connection with being able to hear what God is saying to us, that glorifying Jesus is a distinctive mark of the Holy Spirit. Many things that are said to be the work of the Holy Spirit in the charismatic movement lack the mark of glorifying Jesus. Anything that exalts a human personality is not from the Holy Spirit. It may be spiritual, but it is not from the Holy Spirit. Whatever the Spirit does, His ultimate aim is always to glorify Jesus. If Jesus is not center stage, the scenario is not from the Holy Spirit.

YIELDING TO GOD'S CHOICE

Although all the functions of the head are important, I want to briefly focus on the fourth function—to coordinate the activity of the members, who carry out the decisions of the head—in regard to our relationship with Christ. This deals with the issue of initiative.

Jesus said to His disciples in John 15:16, *"You did not choose Me, but I chose you."* This statement is very clear; there is no doubt about it. I don't think Jesus was referring to the choice for salvation in this verse, but rather the choice for apostleship. He said, "I have chosen you Twelve."

Jesus continued, *"And appointed you* [or placed you] *that you should go and bear fruit, and that your fruit should remain"* (verse 16). I understand from this that the only enduring fruit proceeds out of the choice of God. You can have all sorts of religious programs and activities and elections in the church, but if God didn't initiate them, there will be no permanent fruit whatever.

Jesus also said, *"That whatever you ask the Father in My name He may give you"* (John 15:16). Do you understand that the ability to pray effectively to the Father proceeds from the will of God? We can pray all sorts of prayers, but if they do not proceed from the will of God, we have no assurance that He will answer them. My impression is that God is urgently dealing with the church in the United States to bring us back to a realization of our total dependence on Him.

So, initiative is expressed through choice, and as I understand it, the only aspects of our lives God is really involved in are those He has chosen. Any time we take the initiative out of the hands of God, we have shut off the headship of Jesus. We have actually been extremely presumptuous. May God forgive us. Basically, I think the church is going to have to

> *Holy Spirit*
>
> To go into the future without the Holy Spirit's guidance is to head toward disaster.

get on its face before God and say, "Lord, we have been totally arrogant. We repent and ask You to forgive us."

A good example of dependence on God's choice is in the book of Acts:

> *Now in the church that was at Antioch there were certain prophets and teachers: Barnabas, Simeon who was called Niger, Lucius of Cyrene, Manaen who had been brought up with Herod the tetrarch, and Saul. As they ministered to the Lord and fasted, the Holy Spirit said, "Now separate to Me Barnabas and Saul for the work to which I have called them."*
>
> (Acts 13:1–2)

The *New International Version* says, *"While they were worshiping the Lord and fasting."* I read the original Greek in this way: "As they conducted their priestly ministry to the Lord." They could have been worshiping, or they could have been doing something else. But while they were waiting on the Lord, without any agenda of their own, the Holy Spirit said, in effect, "This is My agenda."

How many times does the church come to God with its own agenda and never once ask Him, "What is Your will?" You can't make your decisions, write them out in the minutes of the church meeting, and then apply the name of God as a rubber stamp, because God is not a rubber stamp. He is almighty God.

The Scripture passage continues, *"Then, having fasted and prayed, and laid hands on them, they sent them away"* (Acts 13:3). Where did the decision to send out Paul and Barnabus come from? It came from God by the Holy Spirit.

Before these men were sent out by the Holy Spirit, they were prophets and teachers. What were they after they were sent out? *Apostles.* Note that they are called apostles twice:

> *But the multitude of the city was divided: part sided with the Jews, and part with the apostles.* (Acts 14:4)

> *But when the apostles Barnabas and Paul heard this....* (Acts 14:14)

An apostle is one who is sent forth, so anybody who has not been sent forth cannot be an apostle. Interestingly, although the initiative proceeded from God the Father, by Jesus Christ the Son, through the Holy Spirit, they were not called apostles before the church had sent them out. God does not bypass the church in appointing ministries.

When Paul and Barnabas concluded this particular ministry assignment, it says, *"From there they sailed to Antioch, where they had been commended to the grace of God for the work which they had completed"* (Acts 14:26). How many of us in the church today can say that we have completed the work that we were assigned? Not just done part of it but completed the whole job? My explanation for their fulfilling their assignment is that the initiative proceeded from God. The leaders of the church at Antioch heard and followed His choice. Anything else will not produce the same results.

HAVING THE MIND OF CHRIST

An important part of learning to hear God's voice is understanding that the church has *"the mind of Christ"* (1 Corinthians 2:16). Paul, quoting from Isaiah 40:13–14, wrote, *"Who has known the mind of the LORD that he may instruct Him?"* (1 Corinthians 2:16). How many of us are in a position to instruct the Lord? To give Him advice? To tell Him how to do things? This is a rhetorical question. The answer is nobody. Paul continued, *"But we have the mind of Christ"* (verse 16). Note that the Scripture says "we," not "I," have the mind of Christ. The mind of Christ is not given to one single individual; it is given to the body by the Head. Until the members of the body learn to understand the mind of Christ together, it will go largely undiscovered.

Can you say regarding your particular church or fellowship, "We have the mind of Christ"? Would you even contemplate that question? Does it occur to you that we *should* be able to say that?

WAITING ON GOD CHANGES US

How can we become people who truly have the mind of Christ? I believe there is a very simple, one-word answer. It is a very unpopular word among American Christians, the word we least like to hear: *Wait*. Not work, but wait.

In 1 Thessalonians, Paul was writing to some of the earliest Christians. In fact, this is probably one of the first letters he ever wrote to the churches. In commenting on the impact of the gospel in Thessalonica, he said,

> *For they themselves declare concerning us what manner of entry we had to you, and how you turned to God from idols to serve the living and true God, and to wait for His Son from heaven.*
>
> (1 Thessalonians 1:9–10)

Notice that they *"turned to God"* to do two things: (1) serve, and (2) wait. That is the totality of the Christian life. Serving is not all of it. In fact, it is very incomplete if it is not accompanied by waiting. We serve, and we wait. In more than fifty places, the Bible speaks about the necessity of waiting on God or for God. Isaiah 64:4 in the *New International Version* is so vivid: *"Since ancient times no one has heard, no ear has perceived, no eye has seen any God besides you, who acts on behalf of those who wait for him."*

In this picture of the one true God, what is His distinctive characteristic? He acts on behalf of those who wait for Him. If you want Him to act on your behalf, you have to wait. My strong conviction is that the church is never going to get beyond where it is today until it learns to wait on God.

I conducted a series of meetings in a small city in England called Hull. At the end of these meetings, I called the leaders up on the platform and prayed for them. Apparently, God released something through that prayer because, for four years afterward, this group of leaders representing perhaps fifteen churches met together and waited on God. Then they invited me

Holy Spirit

The totality of the Christian life can be summed up like this: turn to God, serve, and wait.

back, and this second series of meetings was different from almost any other meetings I have ministered in. It wasn't that I had changed. Something about the atmosphere there had changed.

I preached some very straightforward messages about how only those sins we confess are forgiven. If we do not confess our sins, they are not forgiven. God is fully ready and waiting to forgive, but He has laid down a condition: *"If we confess our sins, He is faithful and just to forgive us our sins and to cleanse us from all unrighteousness"* (1 John 1:9).

About ten couples responded to the message by coming forward to the front. Without any emotion or hype, I said to the whole group, "Now, if you need to confess sins, you can confess them to God. But the Bible also says, *'Confess your sins to each other and pray for each other so that you may be healed'* (James 5:16 NIV). You're free to come down and do that." They came down for about two hours, one by one, to confess their sins. And some of them were quite well known leaders in that area.

I see this response as the fruit of people waiting on God. I hear a lot of prophecies about revival, and I may have given some myself. But we will not have revival until we have met the conditions. You can prophesy as much as you like, but the real barrier to revival is unconfessed sin. Until that has been dealt with, you can publicize meetings and preach and sing—but the results will be disappointing.

You may say, "I don't think I have any sins to confess." Well, wonderful! But how close are you to God? After you spend a little while waiting in the presence of God, you may have a different perspective. I am sharing out of personal experience. I have never been a "backslider." I have served the Lord for more than fifty years, and by the grace of God I have seen countless numbers of people helped. But when Ruth and I got alone with God without any premeditated plan or agenda, it took God six months to clear up the debris in my life. God showed me things I had done thirty years previously, and said, "You never confessed it." And just to help us humble ourselves, Ruth and I confessed to one another. You don't always have to do that, but the Bible does say to confess your sins to one another.

I read in the journals of John Wesley that somewhere in Yorkshire, England, one of the strongest Methodist societies had grown out of the commitment of people who met together weekly to confess their faults to one another. That is not the modern plan for starting a church, is it? But, after all, the Methodist movement did impact the whole of Britain and most of the United States for a century. So, maybe there is something to be said for this approach.

Let me point out that many people desire physical healing, yet that is not God's number one priority. Some people in those meetings in Yorkshire were instantly healed when they forgot about healing and determined to get right with God. The psalmist David said, in effect, "My sins have mounted up over my head and are a burden to me." (See Psalm 32:1–6; 51:1–4.) Many of you would like to be healed, but you will never be healed until you have dealt with the sin problem in your life.

Isaiah 59:1 says, *"Behold, the LORD's hand is not short-ened, that it cannot save; nor His ear heavy, that it cannot hear."* We are so used to refer-ring these words to the Jews that we sometimes forget they also apply to Gentiles. God still has good hearing, and His arm still is powerful. Yet verse two says, *"But your iniquities have sepa-rated you from your God; and your sins have hid-den His face from you, so that He will not hear."*

> *Holy Spirit*
>
> God still has good hearing. Confessing and forsaking our sins reopens the channel to Him.

God does not show partiality. It is wonderful to know that we have the right of access to God through the blood of Jesus when the blood of Jesus cleanses us. But the blood does not cleanse those who do not confess. *"If we walk in the light as He is in the light, we have fellowship with one another, and the blood of Jesus Christ His Son cleanses us from all sin"* (1 John 1:7). Three continuing present tense words are included in this verse. If we *continually* walk in the light, we *continually* have fellowship one with another, and the blood *continually* cleanses. But they are conditional. The first word is *if.* *"If we walk in the light."*

If we are not in fellowship, we are not in the light. And if we are out of fellowship, the blood is not cleansing us. The blood does not cleanse in the dark; it only cleanses in the light. If we have been in the dark and want to be cleansed, we have to come to the light. My personal opinion is that God will never have His way with the church in America until the leaders of the church take time to wait on God. I say specifically the *leaders.*

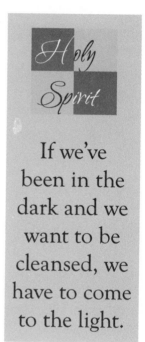

Holy Spirit

If we've been in the dark and we want to be cleansed, we have to come to the light.

I would like to conclude this chapter with an account from a friend of mine, a well-known minister named Johannes Facius, of the International Fellowship of Intercessors. He wrote a newsletter about something that happened in Australia. The Aussies are a pretty tough crowd, I think you will agree, and a spiritual breakthrough in Australia would be a remarkable event. And, I believe it is coming. I hope this account will encourage you.

A couple of days ago I returned from the ends of the earth, Australia, and the most unique gathering of spiritual leaders I have ever attended. After this experience I will never be the same again. [And he's a man of mature ministry and experience.]

Noel Bell, Intercessors for Australia, and Tom Hallas, leader of YWAM in Australia [I know them both], had felt the need to call together pastors, elders, and leaders of ministries from all over Australia to come together to seek the face of the Lord. The conference was called "Leaders Looking unto Jesus," and the time frame was three weeks. This in itself was a daring step. How could anyone imagine it being possible for busy spiritual leaders to set aside three whole weeks? When I realized that more than one hundred had responded to this call and saw that most of them stayed for the whole period, I was convinced that it had to be one of the seven wonders of this world. Had anyone proposed to me to do something like this in Europe or the States I would have laughed at the thought. If we can get leaders together here for a whole day we ought to be grateful. Apparently God must have something special in mind with Australia, and I would not be surprised if a very powerful spiritual awakening would come out of Australia and touch the worldwide body of Christ.

Possibly it is the isolation that our Australian friends feel out there at the edge of the globe, coupled with a realization of the hardness and roughness of the Australian heart, that have been the main factors moving our friends to cast themselves down before the Lord. At any rate, no matter how far I go back in living memory I have not been a part of anything like this before in my years in the ministry. So let me enlighten you with some of the extraordinary things that took place.

LEARNING TO HEAR *God's Voice*

Sitting at His Feet

This was the way God laid out the purpose of this gathering: to sit at His feet like Mary and not, like Martha, try to please Him and serve Him by our own initiative. To enter into His rest, which is the rest from our own works, just as God, having created heaven and earth in six days, rested from His works on the seventh. This proved to be very difficult for all of us. Whenever we tried to sit silently in His presence, only five minutes would pass and someone would not be able to wait any longer but had to break in with a prophecy or a song or a Scripture reading. All proving how hard it is for us to wait and let the Spirit take the initiative. Praise God we had lots of time before us, three whole weeks. And slowly but surely we learned to just wait until the Spirit would begin to blow with His gentle wind among us. How difficult it is for us to just enjoy God's presence without exercising any kind of activity.

Beholding His Glory

Second Corinthians 3:18 became very much alive to us. *"But we all, with unveiled face, beholding as in a mirror the glory of the Lord, are being transformed into the same image from glory to glory, just as by the Spirit of the Lord."* Coming under the entire lordship of the Holy Spirit is equal to coming face-to-face with Jesus. [This is exactly what I have desired to communicate to you in this chapter.] In the light of His glory and perfection we can measure ourselves, in all our shortcomings, and be exposed to the transforming power of His Spirit changing us into the image of His dear Son. How different this way is to our own attempts at looking at ourselves and despair over all that is lacking of Christ-likeness in our character. God had called us together not as we had expected, to load on us new knowledge and information, but to change us into the likeness of His dear Son.

The Vertical Way

For me personally a change took place in my whole thinking. As one who has been active in the prayer movement for more than twenty years, I had developed a way of discerning problems and places by help from the information available and using my analytical mind. By looking unto Jesus and waiting to come face-to-face with Him, I discovered that any true discernment of any situation only comes when we look at it through His face. If we want a true picture of ourselves, we need to see ourselves the way He looks upon us. If we want to know where the church is standing and how the situation is in our very own nation, we can look at it at the horizontal level and measure it by the outward appearances, but we would end with a wrong and untrue picture. Only as we behold the face of the Lord and come to understand His burden for His church and His world can we apply our prayers or ministries with great effect.

Falling in Love with Jesus

When people give themselves to seeking the Lord over a three-week period, one would expect that they would end up by being drawn into intimacy with Him. And so it was. The overall discovery of this time was a deep realization of how far away from our first love and from the centrality of Christ we had been used to living our lives—even as His servants. Therefore, the calling was to enter into the bridal chamber and to fall in love with our heavenly Bridegroom, to return to our first love and make Jesus the center and focus of everything we were doing. And so it happened. As He went on exposing His great and strong love to us, we yielded more and more to Him, and the joy and the worship increased in quality and strength. At the end, whole sessions were spent just reveling in His love. We had lost any ambition of being effective and wanted only to be with Him more and more. The Song of Solomon, with its many rich pictures of the developing love relationship between the bride and the bridegroom, became a guideline for us all the way through. I know that I am using big words when I say that nothing so far in my life can compare with these weeks. But I'm convinced that no matter how big such a statement might sound, it is the truth. And as I am writing this newsletter I have a strong desire in my heart to be allowed to continue in this direction, looking unto Jesus. This is also what I wish for all of God's people, that they would have the great joy of being a part of such a gathering in the nearest future.[1]

---

[1] From *International Fellowship of Intercessors Newsletter,* September 1992, based on author's verbal rendering. Used by permission.

I include this account because I want to move out of the realm of theory and into the realm of practical experience. That is an example of what happens when people take time to wait on God.

If you feel there is a barrier between you and God, that there are things that come between the Lord and you in your life, and that you are not hearing from God the way you wish, it is time to come to Him and wait on Him. You can confess these things and be free of them, and get clear in your relationship with Him.

I conclude by reemphasizing this truth: the way to live as a real son of God is to be led regularly by the Holy Spirit. It is exactly as Jesus said, *"My sheep **hear** My voice, and I know them, and they **follow** Me"* (John 10:27, emphasis added). The life of the Spirit means regularly hearing and regularly following. It is not an up and down, sporadic process. It is a regular, continuing relationship with our heavenly Father, through His Son Jesus Christ, by the Holy Spirit.

ABOUT THE
Author

ABOUT THE AUTHOR

*D*erek Prince (1915–2003) was born in Bangalore, India, into a British military family. He was educated as a scholar of classical languages (Greek, Latin, Hebrew, and Aramaic) at Eton College and Cambridge University in England and later at Hebrew University, Israel. As a student, he was a philosopher and self-proclaimed atheist. He held a fellowship in ancient and modern philosophy at King's College, Cambridge.

While in the British Medical Corps during World War II, Prince began to study the Bible as a philosophical work. Converted through a powerful encounter with Jesus Christ, he was baptized in the Holy Spirit a few days later. This life-changing experience altered the whole course of his life, which he thereafter devoted to studying and teaching the Bible as the Word of God.

Discharged from the army in Jerusalem in 1945, he married Lydia Christensen, founder of a children's home there. Upon their marriage, he immediately became father to Lydia's eight adopted daughters—six Jewish, one Palestinian Arab, and one English. Together, the family saw the rebirth of the state of Israel in 1948. In the late 1950s, the Princes adopted another daughter while he was serving as principal of a college in Kenya.

In 1963, the Princes immigrated to the United States and pastored a church in Seattle. Stirred by the tragedy of John F. Kennedy's assassination, he began to teach Americans how to intercede for their nation. In 1973, he became one of the founders of Intercessors for America. His book *Shaping History through Prayer and Fasting* has awakened Christians around the world to their responsibility to pray for their governments. Many consider underground translations of the book as instrumental in the fall of communist regimes in the USSR, East Germany, and Czechoslovakia.

Lydia Prince died in 1975, and Derek married Ruth Baker (a single mother to three adopted children) in 1978. He met his second wife, like his first, while he was serving the Lord in Jerusalem. Ruth died in December 1998 in Jerusalem, where they had lived since 1981.

Until a few years before his own death in 2003 at the age of eighty-eight, Prince persisted in the ministry God had called him to as he traveled the world, imparting God's revealed truth, praying for the sick and afflicted, and sharing his prophetic insights into world events in the light of Scripture.

He is the author of more than fifty books, many of which have been translated and published in more than one hundred languages. His radio program, now known as *Derek Prince Legacy Radio*, began in 1979 and has been translated into over a dozen languages. Derek's main gift of explaining the Bible and its teaching in a clear, simple way has helped build a foundation of faith in millions of lives. His nondenominational, nonsectarian approach has made his teaching equally relevant and helpful to people from all racial and religious backgrounds, and his teaching is estimated to have reached more than half the globe.

Internationally recognized as a Bible scholar and spiritual patriarch, Derek Prince established a teaching ministry that spanned six continents and more than sixty years. In 2002, he said, "It is my desire—and I believe the Lord's desire—that this ministry continue the work, which God began through me over sixty years ago, until Jesus returns."

With its international headquarters in Charlotte, North Carolina, Derek Prince Ministries continues to reach out to believers in over 140 countries with Derek's teaching, fulfilling the mandate to keep on "until Jesus returns." This is accomplished through the outreaches of more than thirty Derek Prince Ministries International offices around the world, including primary work in Australia, Canada, China, France, Germany, the Netherlands, New Zealand, Norway, Russia, South Africa, Switzerland, the United Kingdom, and the United States. For current information about these and other worldwide locations, visit www.derekprince.org.

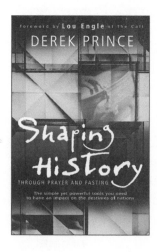

Shaping History through Prayer & Fasting
Derek Prince

The times we are living in are scary, to say the least, yet what we are facing isn't new. History is replete with violent episodes of unimaginable carnage and terror. And what did people do about them? The only thing they could do—they prayed! Best-selling author Derek Prince reveals how your prayers can make a real difference right now and into the future. Discover how to touch the heart of God through effective fasting and prayer—prayer that will change the world!

ISBN: 978-0-88368-773-4 • Trade • 192 pages

Faith to Live By
Derek Prince

The dynamics, the promises, the power of faith—all are explored in this insightful book. Derek Prince answers your questions about faith and explains how you can immediately receive what you pray for, obtain spiritual gifts, enjoy abundant life, and hear what God is saying to you. Discover techniques that will build your faith in God and empower you to do what would otherwise be impossible. Easy to read and based on the Scriptures, *Faith to Live By* is a resource for every Christian who wants to receive the promises of a faith-filled life.

ISBN: 978-0-88368-519-8 • Trade • 192 pages

WHITAKER
HOUSE

Self-Study Bible Course, Expanded Edition
Derek Prince

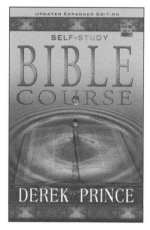

If you have questions about God and the Bible, here is the help you need. In this Bible study course, you will find answers to questions such as, "How can I have victory over sin?" and "How can I receive answers to my prayers?" If you have never read the Bible before, you will find this systematic study guide easy to use and helpful. Or, if you have been a believer for many years, you will find a new ease in conversing with God, fellowshipping with Christians, and witnessing and winning souls. This expanded edition provides an in-depth exploration of topics such as healing and guidance.

ISBN: 978-0-88368-750-5 • Workbook • 216 pages

Derek Prince on Experiencing God's Power
Derek Prince

In this anointed collection of several of his best-selling books, Derek Prince shows how to receive God's promises regarding healing, fasting, marriage, spiritual warfare, finances, prayer, the Holy Spirit, and many others. By utilizing the scriptural principles outlined in this book, you will discover answers to some of life's toughest issues, including how to impact world events, how to know God's will for your life, how to use God's powerful weapons to fight evil, and how to overcome rejection, betrayal, and shame. Here is a unique and valuable guide for helping you achieve powerful results in your spiritual quest.

ISBN: 978-0-88368-551-8 • Trade • 528 pages

WHITAKER
HOUSE

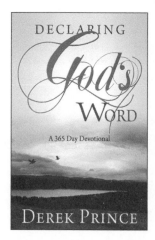

Declaring God's Word:
A 365-Day Devotional
Derek Prince

According to Scripture, Satan can be defeated if believers will stand on God's Word and testify to what it says about the mighty and powerful blood of Jesus—blood that cleanses us from sin and makes us righteous. For the first time, acclaimed Bible teacher Derek Prince will lead you to power and victory in this yearlong daily devotional. By *Declaring God's Word*, you will become steeped in the Scriptures and overcome satanic oppression and attacks. Begin each new day by confessing the truth of God's Word, and you will experience the love, power, and wisdom of God all year long.

ISBN: 978-1-60374-067-8 • Trade • 432 pages

Power in the Name
Derek Prince

God deeply desires to have a relationship of love with His people. Best-selling author and Bible teacher Derek Prince helps you uncover the character and divine power of God by exploring many of His names and titles, including "The One Who Provides," "The One Who Heals," and "The Prince of Peace." As you delve into the nature of God, you will find true peace and security, as you discover your purpose in life. And remember, God the Father loves you as much as He loves His Son, Jesus. (See John 17:23.) As you learn the attributes of God and get to know Him more intimately, you will reap the blessings of His many promises and have your deepest needs met.

ISBN: 978-1-60374-067-8 • Trade • 176 pages

WHITAKER
HOUSE